44 Secrets for Great Soccer Goalie Skills

Mirsad Hasic

ISBN: 1492709379
ISBN-13: 978-1492709374

DEDICATION

I dedicate this book all soccer players around the world.

CONTENTS

ACKNOWLEDGMENTS

I would like to thank my family for their support.

1 ORGANIZING A COUNTERATTACK

OK, so you've saved an amazing shot and feel you've done a great job, that is, prevent the opponents from scoring. Now you are standing there holding the ball as you try to figure out which player to pass it to.

If you've got this far then you've probably wasted a good chance for creating a scoring opportunity. But hold on a minute!

Haven't you just saved a dangerous shot from getting into the net?

Sure you have, and so you deserve some praise here, not criticism, right?

Well, this hesitation is what separates the amateur goalkeeper from professional. The moment a save has been made, it is the goalie's responsibility to immediately look at where his teammates are positioned and make a spontaneous and informed decision of where to pass the ball next.

In my experience, opponents tend to be at their most vulnerable after a failed offensive attack. What this means is that they will be out of their defending positions, and that gives you an ideal chance to reinstate a quick counterattack.

The general rule here is the faster you can put the ball back in play to an unmarked teammate, the chances of succeeding with the counterattack increase. In other words, the quicker you get up and throw or kick the ball to an unmarked teammate, the better.

It is very important to realize that your throw or kick must be as accurate as possible. Be aware too that the further the distance is to the player, the chance of failure becomes higher.

Another important aspect is the weather. You will need to adapt to whatever the conditions is at the time. There are other things you will need to take into consideration too, such as the skills of your individual teammates, and your own ability to pass the ball with accuracy, etc.

For example, if the soccer field is wet don't throw the ball with power and spin. If you do, the moment it lands the ball will gain more pace and your teammate will find it hard to get it under control.

I used to play with a keeper that had amazing reflexes. This guy could save just about anything while he was on the goal line.

However, his footwork was really poor. This meant that counterattacks were not really an option because he would just kick the ball out of play.

Ask yourself in all honestly whether you consider your foot skills to be solid or something that perhaps need working on.

If you are not completely sure, then put some time into improving this area. Believe me when I say that kicking with accuracy is really important for succeeding as a modern-day goalie.

To summarize, I want you to remember that being able to quickly organize a counterattack after a successful save is one of the most important skills you need in order to become a great goalkeeper.

2 FOCUS 100%

Being a goalkeeper is somewhat different compared to the rest of the team. Field players may lose focus for a while without being negatively affected, whereas a second of lost focus as a goalkeeper could lose the team their victory.

Maintaining focus can be easier said than done because it often depends on the level of competition you are facing. In other words, the higher the competition the more natural focus you will have.

A game at a lower level, however, or one where you team keeps the ball down the other end of the field, may become mundane for a goalie, and that can result in a loss of concentration.

I am aware of that with some of your games you may feel your presence is completely meaningless, and that you are there simply to make the numbers up.

I've seen keepers performing catastrophically against weak opponents and making rookie mistakes because they lost all momentum during a match where there input - had until that moment - been minimal at best.

So, the question here is this: how do you actually maintain focus at maximum level during games where the opponents are weaker, so that you can step up to the challenge if and when you're required to?

Well, there is a simple strategy that is highly effective at helping you keep maximum focus no matter what level of competition you are facing at any given time.

The idea is to treat every one of your games as if it were a final, and where the outcome decides who will get knocked out of the competition. By doing this you will be able to change your mindset and successfully get comfortable with performing at your best.

If you have been stuck in the "unfocused" mode for a while, then it will probably take you some time to adopt the full-focus mode, but it can be done quite easily providing you are willing.

Use this new way of thinking during practice sessions too. Treat every game like your life depends on it and you will soon start to experience your position with more concentration and energy.

The more ambition you have with your soccer career, the easier you will find it to get into the maximum focus mode.

However, if you are just playing soccer as a part-time hobby, then it will be much harder to maintain constant focus during those quieter games.

I've played in both amateur teams and professional ones, and the difference is huge. Quite often, the practice sessions and games within amateur teams can often resemble something of a ragtag outfit, whereas within a professional team it's totally the opposite.

With pro players, the atmosphere is one in which the team are always juiced-up, completely focused, and ready to compete.

However, don't let your amateur status keep you from thinking like a pro.

To become a professional you have to start thinking like one, so remember to work on staying focused to the max no matter what!

Heck, you might get drafted tomorrow and be thrown into big games immediately, so prepare yourself as if this is a probability.

To summarize this chapter, I would like you to remember that in order to become a successful goalkeeper and reach a higher level of competition, then you really need to maintain maximum focus both during practice and the actual games!

3 SETTING UP REALISTIC GOALS

Most keepers have targets they want to reach, but not all are able to set up realistic goals that are achievable in the short to mid-term. Because of this, a lot of goalkeepers tend to give up on their ambitions and just continue to play without having any real plans.

From my observations, this is perhaps the biggest reason why goalkeepers stop developing their skills.

They simply come to the conclusion that following specific objectives doesn't work well because they don't get the opportunity to reach them within any anticipated timeframe.

You would be amazed at how much your development is diminished by abandoning goals and just playing on without any real ambition.

However, seeing as you've bought my book and come this far, then I assume you are not one of those goalies who plan to quit any time soon.

So, just how does one actually set up realistic goals and avoid getting discouraged should they not be reached in the anticipated timeframe? The answer is actually in the question.

By that, I mean if you've set up a goal and not been able to reach it in the time you expected to, then the goal is most probably unrealistic.

While there could be other issues such as personal problems, injuries, poor coaching and so on, try to use these as explanations and not as excuses.

You must remind yourself that success comes with some failure along the way, and that all the great keepers before you would have faced similar setbacks, yet they still went on to become great goalies nonetheless.

Another thing to consider is to put an "estimated" time, as opposed to a fixed time, on when you should reach a specific goal.

This approach will take the pressure off and help you to monitor progress easier and evaluate possible pitfalls along the way. This in turn will allow you to sharpen your objectives and focus only on the important aspects.

You are probably wondering how to actually set up a realistic amount of time for achieving a specific goal? Well, this is really down to the individual, but personally I prefer to set up a series of smaller goals rather than one big one.

Working with a bite-sized goal is also easier to reach and therefore helps to keep momentum going.

For example, let's assume you want to completely stop the opponents from scoring past you in a game. Instead of setting up a goal where you expect to achieve this in every contest, you have aim instead to achieve it every third match, for instance.

It is unrealistic to think that you will be able to prevent the opponents from scoring in each and every game you play.

By setting up a more realistic plan where you aim to achieve your objective for every one in three games, then your chances of succeeding are far greater. This approach will not only afford you a sense of accomplishment, but it will also help to build on the momentum.

This is just one example of how to create goals that are achievable in a reasonable amount of time.

It's natural to want to be the best you can be in the shortest time possible, but it's far more beneficial in the long run to pace yourself sensibly than it is to just attack something with impatience and idealistic ambition.

Those who do rush in headfirst and with unrealistic expectations are usually the ones to fall down the hardest and most likely the first ones to quit.

4 IDENTIFY & IMPROVE YOUR WEAKNESSES

I know it can be really tough to expose your weaknesses, but this is a necessary thing to do if you are serious about improving your goalkeeping skills. A smart goalie knows this and is therefore not afraid to own up to his flaws and work at improving them.

The quickest way to identify your weak sides is to grab a notebook, sit down somewhere quiet, and start to jot down where you think your vulnerabilities lie. Don't be afraid to be constructively critical with yourself.

Honesty and openness is the only way you will get to improve your game.

Remember, the point of this exercise is not to hurt your ego or put yourself down, but to help you become the best you can be.

After you have written down the areas in which you think could use some improvements, you then need to number them from 1-5, with one being the skill that needs the least improvement, and five being the one with the highest priority.

In other words, the higher the number, the sooner you need to start working on improving that particular skill.

To help you out on this I have created a small template to show how such a list might look. Feel free to modify it to suit your own needs.

1. Improve diving and reaction speed with my non-prominent arm. [5]
2. Increase the distance of my goal kick by more than fifteen yards. [3]
3. Get more comfortable with organizing my teammates in defense. [5]
4. Practice on scoring from penalty kicks in the event of a penalty shoot-out. [2]
5. Learn how to bend the ball and score goals from direct free kicks. [1]

As you can see, I have given each of these areas a specific number depending on its priority.

This is just an example of how you can arrange the skills you want to improve on, but feel perfectly free to use any other method if you find something that might work better for you personally.

What is important to bear in mind here is that you must be completely honest with yourself and not let pride or denial stop you from taking a good look at your skillset in a constructive, and when necessary, a critical way.

Understand that no one will do this for you, so the more transparent you are the more success you will have with this assignment.

Once you have completed your shortlist and arranged the areas to practice on from one to five, you then need to start working on them immediately. Remember, these are fundamental for enhancing your overall performance.

I recommend you tell your coach what you are doing and why. The reason for this is because a coach will more than likely help you by setting some specific drills for you to practice on in the areas that need work.

As you have probably realized already, you need to carry a lot of personal responsibility for your own development.

This is often the case with goalies as the coach is usually overwhelmed with instructing the outfield players during practice sessions, meaning he will not always have time to work with you individually.

5 ALWAYS WATCH THE BALL

Over the years I have noticed how a lot of goalkeepers fail to monitor the path of the ball. Instead, they spend way too much time trying to organize the defense, or they concern themselves with what a coach is shouting from the sidelines. While keeping an eye on things like the above is important, you would be amazed how many keepers make the mistake of focusing on the wrong distraction at the wrong time, and not watching the ball as they should be.

I specifically remember one game where I witnessed what can only be described as a classic example of what happens when a keeper is not monitoring the ball. I am hoping you won't make the same mistake after reading this book. OK, here's what happened.

Several years ago I played with a goalkeeper who served as a great example on how NOT to behave when opponents are in possession of the ball and approaching the goal. This goalie felt a little thirsty, so he decided to grab the water bottle that was close to one of his goal posts.

The opponents saw what he was doing and seized the opportunity by firing a cross from 30 yards that landed neatly in the opposite corner.

Our keeper turned around and wondered what had just happened! Needless to say he was scorned by the rest of us because of his haphazard approach to being in goal.

It actually took him few minutes to fully understand what had just occurred. In fact, he even wrongly accused the referee of misconduct.

He thought, the ref had blown his whistle to give a free kick, and said that he merely took the moment to re-hydrate his body. He told the ref that he should not have allowed the kick to take place until he was back in position. It wasn't long before we put him right and let the embarrassment serve as his punishment.

Fortunately we still won the game with a 5-1 victory despite the keeper's blunder. If only he had stayed focused throughout the game and watched the ball, then he would never have been forced to experience the humiliation and disappointment from me and the rest of the team.

At the next practice we were all still making fun of the goalie, such is the banter of a soccer team.

We made sketches of him drinking water while the ball was flying toward the net, but like most players that get the mocked from time to time, he took it all in good spirits and promised to work on improving his game.

However, if we had lost that game as a result of his blunder, then our reaction would have been a lot different and he would have faced way more serious criticism.

After all, a team sport is no good unless the "team" is working as one, but because we triumphed despite of him, we didn't have to face the humiliation of a loss.

To summarize, you must always be mindful to monitor the ball in the first instance. All other distractions should be considered secondary. If you get into the habit of doing this, I can guarantee the ball will pass you much less often than you're used to seeing it!

6 MAKING YOURSELF BIG IN ONE-TO-ONE

Another big mistakes goalkeeper's make is to stand on the goal line as an opponent is approaching them in a one-on-one duel.

Why? Well, put simply, standing on the goal line means that your chances of saving the ball are minimal.

To help you realize how doomed you are by staying on the goal line, I would say that saving a penalty is easier than saving a ball while standing on this spot.

In other words, this is a really poor strategy for beating your opponent, and one that usually ends in your failure to make a save.

I hope I have convinced you that standing on the goal line is something to always avoid in one-on-one duels. So let's now focus on what you can do in order to beat an opponent and win a one-on-one duel.

The best thing you can do when an opponent is approaching you in a one-to-one duel is to run at him, stretch out your whole body as much as possible, and then attack the ball with sheer determination.

By approaching like this you will be able to cut off more angles and also make yourself appear bigger.

In general, the closer you get to the opponent the bigger you will become in his eyes, thus forcing him to make hasty and potentially wrong decisions, which then increases your chances of saving the ball.

The negative side of this strategy is that you will usually only get one chance to save the ball.

If you hit the opponent's leg instead of the ball, then you will either cause a penalty or earn a red card and get sent off the field.

Even so, you will not have much choice in the matter. If you keep standing on the goal line without attacking the opponent and putting pressure on him to make hasty decisions, then there's a real danger that he will succeed in his attempt to score and you will fail in your attempt to save.

Saving a ball in one-to-one situation is a pretty tough challenge. As mentioned previously, you only have one chance to succeed. This means that if you time your attack just a couple of seconds too late, the outcome will most likely not be in your favor.

Don't fear this type of challenge though. It can be done, and the more you do it the better you will become.

A great example on this is the Iker Casillas save on Arjen Robben's shot during the world cup final 2010. This is where he managed to get a foot on the ball despite that he was already going in the wrong direction.

If you have not seen that clip, I suggest you open up YouTube and watch it few times. You will notice that he is standing far from the goal line, making himself appear bigger to the approaching opponents.

It's a tactic that worked so well, it resulted in his team brining the World Cup trophy home to Spain thanks to that courageous save!

7 ANALYZING THE UPCOMING OPPONENTS

I can tell you with certainty that very few amateur goalkeepers take advantage of this strategy and utilize it in their favor.

Professional keepers, on the other hand, study all their opponents carefully before the games in order to learn how they shoot, where they like to aim, and how often they score.

By doing this pre-match analysis, a goalkeeper can work out a strategy in an attempt to prevent the other team from scoring.

There are several ways you can scrutinize the opponents, and as I assume you don't have access to a video library with a plethora of recorded games to fall back on, I will suggest another approach.

All you need to do is find out where your upcoming opponents are playing their next game.

Once you do that, pick a spot on the sidelines from where you are able to observe them without making yourself too obvious.

Be sure to bring a notebook and a pencil along in order to jot down any notes so that you can use to prepare your strategy.

To give you some idea of the kind of things you should be looking out for, I have created a shortlist below. I have outlined the main points that can use to analyze the players.

Once you are done with these, you can implement some of your own ideas as a way to develop your own strategy.

- Find out who is the most dangerous player on the field with regards to scoring goals.
- Does he prefer to shoot with the instep or is he relying on his inside?
- Which is his prominent foot and does he use his non-prominent foot at all? .
- Is he only relying on scoring with his feet or does he try to score using his head as well?
- Count the amount of goals he scored during the game and note how he achieved it/them.

These points are just to get you started. This example gives you some idea on the kind of things you can evaluate as a way of better preparing yourself. You should analyze some of the other opponents as well.

There may actually be other goal scorers in the team you observed that didn't get an opportunity to score on that particular day.

See if you can identify who they might be and take notes of their level of play.

There may be opponents that just happened to have a very good day and score several goals. This is why you should analyze their overall game.

I am telling you this because I once played with a teammate who scored four goals in one single match!

Despite his achievements on that day, his ball skills were really quite poor overall, and the goals he scored were actually the results of rebounds from our best player.

In other words, just because a player has a lucky day, that doesn't necessarily mean you should put too much focus on him.

Getting a good, general idea of a team and the way in which their players play will help improve your chances of saving the day.

This is because you now have some idea of what to expect on the day thanks to observing that team prior to your match against them.

If you are serious about leaving the amateur ranks then you need to behave like a true professional goalkeeper.

That means understanding you opponents and developing an eye for the game in hand.

Because you are reading here, I am quite sure you're aiming for bigger things, so let us continue.

8 AVOIDING HEAD INJURIES

A goalkeeper is often considered to be the bravest player on the team for obvious reasons. However, that doesn't mean he should take unnecessary risks and expose his head to serious injuries.

There are countless examples of goalkeepers who have injured themselves badly, and this is something I want to help you avoid.

From my observations over the years, the most serious injuries occur when a goalie is tired and runs into situations without considering the outcome.

He simply throws himself into the game head-first in the name of the team, and just hopes against hope that he doesn't get kicked in the cranium by attacking opponents as he attempts to save the ball.

This is why you should never, and I really do mean "NEVER," dive headlong into a duel where there is a risk of getting kicked in the head.

There may well be some out there who would praise you for being brave and fearless, but I disagree with encouraging such tactics.

In fact, I would say that it's more stupid than brave because there really is nothing funny about getting seriously injured by taking unnecessary risks. There's plenty of potential for injury in soccer as it is, without inviting danger.

Soccer is a game where you are expected to have fun and keep yourself fit, and to do that you have to take steps to avoid injury.

Even if you have big plans for your soccer career, that doesn't justify diving into situations out of a desperate attempt to get noticed.

In actual fact, if any talent scouts happen to be watching, they may well look at such a method of play as too reckless and risky.

I've seen several keepers quit their soccer careers over the years because of concussions to the brain, and other more permanent damage.

Sadly, almost all of these injuries could have been avoided by lowering the risk of play. The saddest thing of all was that these goalkeepers had many years left to contribute, yet were forced to quit because of their injuries.

I specifically remember this one goalkeeper who was among the top three in our competition.

He was aspiring to be a professional and about to sign a contract with a club that had plans for him to join them at the end of the season.

Sadly, just a few games before the end of season he got kicked in the head and lost consciousness for several minutes.

It was really frightening to see him lying there lifeless. It seemed as though the ambulance was never going to arrive, even though they were on the scene within minutes.

He spent just over a week in hospital and the doctors told him that if he wants to keep living and not risk permanent injuries to his brain, then he would need to quit playing soccer all together, forever!

They said that another blow to the skull like this one could potentially see him paralyzed for the rest of his life.

Although he had a hard time accepting this advice, he still heeded the warnings the doctors had given.

He made a conscious decision there and then to never play soccer again. He eventually became a referee, but he always looked back and spoke passionately on how much he missed playing in goal.

While this is a sad story, you can still learn a lot from it. The lesson is simple: never unnecessarily risk a kick to the head when playing soccer.

As I said before, it is just not worth it. So you need to ask yourself what's more important in life, your long-term health or to save that goal no matter what!

9 BEING SELF CRITICAL

One of the most difficult things to do as goalie is to be transparent and objective when it comes to evaluating your own performance.

The reason for this is because many of us find it much easier to blame someone or something else for our failures.

Over the years I've seen keepers blame their inability to save a goal on teammates, even when everyone else agrees that it was solely the goalies inability to save the shot that let it into the net, and nothing to do with anyone else.

Ego and denial can sometime be the enemy of soccer players, and no one likes to own up to personal defects in their game, but own up we must if we are to progress and become the best that we can be.

So how can you let go of stubborn pride and take more responsibility for your own shortcomings on the soccer pitch? Well, the solution is simple, but that doesn't mean it's going to be easy.

The first thing you should do is to sit down and make a conscious decision never to blame your failures on someone else, even in those cases where it's really not your fault.

The blame game can be justified because it only demoralizes an individual or a team anyway, so what's the point! It's always better to look for potential solutions than it is to focus on the problem.

Try to visualize your own failures and realize that even if Johnny could be blamed for the goal, you should still not blame him for it.

After all, whatever mistake he made out there would not have been intentional. Tell yourself that you are the goalkeeper and if a ball passes you then you are the one who is responsible for letting it in.

The second thing is to identify the situations where mistakes tend to occur. Once you can do that, then you are in a better position to prevent the same things from happening again.

For example, you might discover that you often drop the ball while trying to catch a cross. If so, then you should immediately start working on improving this.

There are probably other situations where you are making mistakes that only become obvious once you start to openly and honestly critique your game. The key here is to go back in time and review your mishaps until you have identified them all.

As soon as you have a clearer picture on the way you perform in any given situation, you can then start working on the skills that will prevent these same blunders from occurring in the future.

The third and final thing is to simulate the mistakes you've made in previous games as a way to test whether you have improved in these areas or not.

For example, jump for the cross again and see if you can catch that ball this time without losing grip on it. If you can, rinse and repeat the exercise until you're confident that you've fixed the problem once and for all.

If you still continue to lose grip, then practice, practice, and practice some more until you've licked it.

As you can probably see, there's a lot of benefit to be had from becoming self-critical, albeit in a constructive way.

A little humility can work wonders for improving you game. It helps you to identify your weak points and then work on correcting them.

The key is to stop hiding behind excuses and avoid blaming failures on someone or something else. Do this and you will get to fast track your development as a goalkeeper.

10 HANDLING THE BALL WITH FEET

Have you ever studied professional goalkeepers and noticed how skillful they are at controlling the ball with their feet?

They seem to be just like any other player on the field as they manage the ball with calm and determination before putting it back into play.

If you have not yet realized this, understand that it's very important to be able to control the ball using the feet with proficiency and confidence if you want to succeed as a goalkeeper.

It doesn't matter what level your other skills are because if you can't control the ball properly with the feet, then any other talents become less useful.

Put short, the best keepers are good "all rounders," i.e. the most effective goalies are also talented players.

In other words, they are able to do more with the ball that just catch it, throw it, and kick it away.

I've played against keepers who were amazing at the goal line but then totally flunked by messing up a backwards pass that landed in the goal.

If I were to pick one skill that separates professional goalkeepers from the amateurs, it would have to be their ability to control the ball with the feet.

Unfortunately, there is no secret formula or shortcuts that will improve your ball control skills. This is something that can only come about through practice.

Whenever you get the chance, play with the ball as much as you can and incorporate this into your regular training sessions.

For example, if you spend say 30 minutes per day working on your catch and throw techniques, allow 10 minutes of these practice sessions to work on foot control skills.

One idea is to use a wall. Walls are great for kicking the ball against and receiving it on the bounce back. By doing this you get to improve your ball receiving skills.

Learning how to receive the ball with your feet, and get it under control, will save the embarrassment of having it off your foot over to an opponent.

Another suggestion for improving ball control skills is to be a field player occasionally.

I understand that as a keen goalie you want to improve your ball handling skills, but you also need to develop and maintain your foot skills too.

Furthermore, participating as a field player from time to time also helps you to get a better overall understanding for the game (something which is priceless for keepers).

How quick you can learn to handle the ball well with your feet depends on several factors. If you have already played soccer on the field, then you already have a head start.

How talented you are overall will also determine how quickly you get to master controlling the ball with your feet.

But most important of all will come down to how much work you are prepared to put into improving in this area.

Those of you who work hard at improving this skill –
regularly – are the ones who will obviously shine.

As a goalkeeper, you really can't afford to make the
mistake of messing up backward passes just because your
ability to control the ball with the feet is below par.

Remember, practice makes perfect!

11 UNDERESTIMATING THE OPPONENTS

I bet you have underestimated your opponents at least once during a game. It's a common mistake, and when we think a player is lacking in skill we tend to become complacent and let our guard down.

Complacency is not something you want to bring with you into a game because it can, and often does, cost your team the match!

The solution therefore, is to treat every opponent equally no matter what you think their abilities are.

By doing this, you will be on your guard at all times during the game.

You will then get into the habit of not taking anyone or any situation for granted, and that can only work in your favor.

To give you a real world example on how dangerous it is to underestimate your opponents, I will share a personal story that still hurts writing about to this day.

I can remember us leading our competition throughout the entire season.

Needless to say we were feeling just great, unstoppable even! As we were on our way to the last game of the season, I recall having a conversation with our goalkeeper.

He said that this game was going to be a piece of cake and that we could win it with our eyes shut. I told him we should never underestimate our opponents, but he refused to listen and said that this game was already in the bag.

The game started well and we scored an early goal. So far so good and everything up to now was going as we had hoped.

However, in the middle of the first half our goalkeeper received a backwards pass. Then, for some strange reason he thought it was a good idea to try dribbling an attacking opponent. He failed miserably!

This opponent then just needed to tap the ball into the goal, and that's exactly what he did do, calmly, and unhurried.

I asked the goalkeeper what he was playing at, but he just smiled and said that the team ought to start scoring more goals instead of jogging around like a bunch of amateurs.

As the game progressed we became ever more nervous, and because of this we started to make a lot of simple mistakes.

We had to score a goal in order to win the competition, but the opponent's keeper was playing the game of his life.

Honestly, this guy was making one great save after another, much to the surprise and frustration of us all.

When there were only a few minutes left in the game our opponents fired a long-range shot.

It seemed pretty harmless at the time, or at least it would have been if our goalie had taken it seriously!

Can you believe he tried to catch the ball with one arm? He failed miserably, and the ball bounced cheekily into the goal.

Now the opposing team had taken the lead and we knew right there and then that it was game over for us.

We not only lost that game, but the competition as well as the second placed team won their match and surpassed us by a single point.

Our goalkeeper started to cry and said that he was really sorry about what he'd done, but it was too late for apologies.

All that was left was to learn from the mistake of underestimating the opponents!

This should give you a picture of what can happen when you underrate your opponent's ability. If you want to become a skillful goalkeeper, you must avoid this mindset at all costs and treat every game seriously.

12 ARGUING WITH TEAMMATES

As a goalkeeper, communicating with your teammates is something you should do often.

Good communication not only helps to prevent opponents from scoring goals, but it also makes your life as a keeper much easier.

Having said that, the type of communication must always be positive and relevant.

Interaction with your fellow teammates can be a powerful tool, but used in the wrong way it can easily turn into something quite negative, like arguing or petty sniping, both of which should be avoided at all costs!

Getting into verbal brawls not only decreases your focus on the game, but it also affects the moral of the other players too.

I've seen this happen many times, and the outcome of a game is rarely positive when bickering is allowed to run rife among a team.

Therefore, I suggest you only communicate with a positive voice and avoid getting into arguments with other players, no matter how much you feel like having a pop at someone about something at the time.

Just remember that maintaining a positive stance throughout a game will help to improve your performance.

Even in those times where you feel it's justified to have a go at someone, just bear in mind that airing your frustration during a match will have no positive effect on you individually or the team as a whole.

I specifically remember a goalkeeper I used to play with once who had a really short fuse. During one game he became so upset that he got into a heated argument with a teammate.

The outcome was that both of these players were sent off because the referee didn't allow such behavior, as most referees don't!

After the game, the coach announced that both the keeper and one of my teammates were suspended because of their behavior on the field.

Besides losing two skillful players, we also had an unbalanced team now because we had to find replacements for them.

At the time of their suspension we were leading our competition with three points.

However, by the end of season we ended up in 7th place because we were forced to use a goalie that was several years younger and much more inexperienced compared to our original one.

I want you to acknowledge that arguing is something that can have a really negative outcome for you and your team.

As you can see from the above account, my team lost a good goalie and one of our star players, and for what? A temper tantrum that lasted for little more than a minute!

And not only did we lose a couple of great team members, but we also lost the whole competition.

We had worked incredibly hard up until that point, yet all our efforts came undone because of a heated squabble mid-game.

So if you ever find yourself in a situation where you are just about to mouth off negatively to someone about something, just take a moment out to pause for thought.

Try to think about the potential consequences of your actions should you decide to let off steam through a slanging match.

Get into the habit of really focusing on your goalkeeping, and move well away from wasting time and energy by trying to decide whose fault it was when something didn't go well.

13 DISTANCE TO GOAL LINE

Your distance to the goal line should be determined by the position of the ball on the field. The further the ball is from the goal, the more distance you are able to be from the goal line. This is why you sometimes see keepers standing on the 18 yard line during matches.

Although standing a good distance from the goal line is something you might feel comfortable with, it can sometimes be a bad decision.

Just one mistake from this position could actually prove disastrous in the event of a successful long range shot from the opposition. So how do you actually maintain a safe distance from the goal line without risking goals from long range shots?

After all, your reason for standing in this position is so that you are ready to face your opponents in one-to-one duels (see chapter 6). The solution is actually quite simple.

The best way to safeguard your position is to decrease the distance from the goal line the closer the ball approaches. This is the only way that you will be able to maintain a safe distance from the goal line while at the same time being ready to challenge an opponent if necessary.

I always like back up my advice with real life experiences, so I will explain how I utilized this strategy to beat one of the best goalkeepers in our region. For this illustration I will go back to a time in my early twenties. I remember it well; we were facing our main rivals in the regional cup final.

It was a tough game with very few scoring opportunities. In fact, the first half ended in 0-0. On the way out to the second half I got an idea to try scoring from a cross immediately from the kick-off. I knew the chances were slim at best, but we had to do something if we were to get ahead.

I decided not to share my plan of action with anyone, especially the coach. I just knew he would get agitated if I told him what I had in mind, and he would undoubtedly order me to forget such a dumb idea.

So anyway, as we were waiting for the referee to blow his whistle, I took a quick look to see where the goalkeeper was positioned.

To my surprise, he was standing on the penalty box line and seemed to be totally unfocused on the kick off. This gave me even more confidence and I could already envisage the cross passing above him as he watched it soar past and into the goal.

As the referee blew his whistle my teammate touched the ball slightly and I fired a straight and accurate cross at the opponent's goal. The ball was only in the air for a few seconds, but it felt like a lifetime. And just as the coach was about to have a go at me, my plucky plan saw the ball land neatly into the goal.

We actually lost that final, but that's a story for another day. My point here is that you should always keep a safe distance between you and the goal line.

As you can see, even the most experienced goalkeepers can get beaten by a good, accurate cross when they're off guard.

14 ORGANIZING DEFENSE

One of your main duties as a goalkeeper is to continually monitor and organize your defense line. This might seem obvious, but you will see many keepers out there who are completely silent and rarely put much effort into organizing their defensive line.

The reason why you should work hard at organizing your defense line is because it's the smart approach. It means you will have much less to do yourself, but also, a good defensive keeps the opponents from succeeding with any scoring opportunities that come their way.

Think about this for a moment. If the opponents get through the defense without too much effort, then their chances of scoring go up.

A poor defense can also result in causing a penalty, or in the worst case, earn you a red card if you are forced to foul an opponent in a desperate attempt to prevent him from scoring.

While you will make your life easier with a well-organized defense line, you will also help those defending to coordinate better and create a more compact, super-efficient defense.

The goalkeeper is the one who has the best view of the whole field, which is why it is natural for him to assume this responsibility.

During my early teen years, I was playing with a goalkeeper who was really great at the goal line. He was blessed with great reflexes and an ability to dive far.

However, you could not count on his help because he barely said a word to anyone during the games.

This reluctance to take charge negatively affected the team's performance as a whole.

I was often forced to receive the ball while facing the wrong way, and unless one of my other teammates shouted across to inform me there was an opponent hot on my heels, I would never know it. After one game I decided to confront the goalie and ask why he was so reluctant to communicate with us during the games.

He paused for a moment, and then he said he felt embarrassed to shout at his teammates and was afraid of how we might react if he did.

I decided then and there that I needed to do something to try and help him to help us as a team.

It was obvious that he was lacking in self-confidence in this area, but we couldn't go on like this. I mean, our performance is being negatively impacted by his reluctance to shout and direct during games.

At the next practice session I spoke with the coach about this, and he also agreed that we have to do something about it otherwise we were never going to grow as a team.

Before practice began, the coach announced that there was to be a short meeting, but refused to say what it was about. He began by praising our goalkeeper, saying that he's really good and how he's an asset to the team.

But he then went on to say that he was also limiting his potential by keeping his mouth shut during the games, and how he could be so much better if only he got over this reluctance to shout out.

The coach said that from now on our goalie is allowed to scream and shout as much as he wants to at the defense (and any other players as well), as long as he does so in a constructive way.

Well, our goalie was delighted to hear this, and you could see the happiness light up in his eyes. It seemed that he just needed an authority figure to guide him on the issue.

Getting the support from the entire team was also a great help at bringing him out of his shell.

At the very next game he started coordinate the defense line like a maestro synchronizes an orchestra.

From that game on our opponents had a much tougher time getting through our defense!

15 ASK SUCCESSFUL KEEPERS FOR TIPS

A great way to instantly boost your performance is to ask successful keepers for their tips and advice. I'm sure there is at least one goalie in your club who you look up to and can approach to ask for suggestions on how to improve your game.

It's always a good idea is to prepare yourself before you approach a goalkeeper and ask his advice.

You want to get as much out of him as possible, and being prepared will save you from forgetting things and pestering him afterwards with one-liners such as: "Oh yeah, another thing I meant to ask you was…"

By the way, try to be specific with your questions. Don't just walk to him and say: "Hey man, what tips can you give me for becoming a better goalie?"

Remember that a broad question will more than likely get you a pretty general answer. Advice such as make sure to practice a lot and listen to the coach, is something you will already know, so this is why it's better to be prepared and be specific.

When it comes to improving ones skills, it's quiet often the little adjustments that can make the biggest difference.

Perhaps you're not performing well with a particular thing, and if so, try to identify what your problem is and then prepare your question(s) for the more experienced goalie.

Just know that he will be in a much better position to pass on his wisdom if you can present him with your problem - specifically. After all, there can be no solutions unless we first understand the problem.

Try to avoid complication and steer clear of waffling on about nothing in particular. In other words, treat this opportunity as prime time and don't attempt to hog the keeper for too long.

If you take this approach, the more likely he will be to offer advice again in the future. I would suggest keeping your questions to five maximum.

I doubt you will have time to write down everything he says, and depending on what you ask and how he responds, there's a chance you might forget some of the tips and suggestions he gives you.

Therefore, and providing he doesn't mind, you might want to record your meeting with him.

Most mobile phones have an inbuilt voice recorder these days, or failing that you might want to purchase a Dictaphone.

Dictaphones are better quality than voice recorders in smartphones as they are made for the specific purpose of recording speech.

They are compact and lightweight too, and can be invaluable tools. They're not only useful for recording others, but also for recording your own notes before you forget.

OK, so to help you out with question prep, I have created a small plan that you can use as a guide. As always, feel free to adapt it to suit your own needs.

There is nothing advanced about this approach, but it shows you what I did when I used the same strategy to improve my skills:

- Get to know who the most successful goalie is in your club and find out when and where they hold their practice sessions.
- Jot down the questions you want to ask (max 5) and try to make them as specific as possible. If you plan to use a voice recorder, make sure it's working before you approach the goalie.
- Pick one day when you can attend the practice and approach the goalie before the session begins. This way you will get a feeling of whether he is open to your Q&A request.
- If he agrees to help you (and there's a very good chance he will), ask whether he minds if you record the session.
- Once you are back home, be sure to listen to his answers again carefully and try to visualize implementing his tips and suggestion in the next practice. When the day arrives, work at applying what you have learned and then evaluate your skills for progress.

As you see, there is nothing particularly innovative with this simple plan.

Even so, it will help you to better prepare what questions to ask on the day. Just remember to keep things short and specific so that you don't take up too much of the goalie's valuable time.

Do it this way and he will be only too happy to offer you more tips in the future.

16 COVERING DANGEROUS ANGLES

Covering angles is one of the fundamental skills for being a competent goalkeeper. By successfully cutting off the angles you will be able to force opponents to choose options that are harder to score from.

I'm sure you have heard people say: "He came across as an absolute giant" during some of the games you've watched.

What this means is that the goalkeeper was able to cover all the angles available for scoring opportunities, which in turn forced the opponents to shoot in less desired directions.

But, what does it mean to actually cover dangerous angles? Well, to give you a simple example of how this works in practice.

OK, let's imagine that an opponent is preparing to fire a shot from the arc of the 18 yard box. Naturally you would move a few yards in the direction of the ball and then wait for the opponent to fire the shot.

However, before doing that you would make sure you have covered the first post thus encouraging him to shoot at the other.

By doing this, you are forcing the opponent to shoot in the direction of the other post which is much more difficult. This is because it requires him to fire a more powerful, well aimed and curved shot if he's to stand any chance of beating you.

Good goalkeeping has a lot to do with being smarter than the opponents and forcing them to make tougher choices.

The more difficult you can make things for them, the fewer opportunities they have for scoring. You might force them to miss the goal altogether, or get to save an attempted shot at the goal with little effort.

However, sometimes there will be an opponent who gets a lucky shot and manages to score even when you have covered all the angles. That's just the way soccer goes sometimes, and the unpredictability of the game is what makes it such an exciting sport.

To give you an example of covering dangerous angles, I always like to use the free kick performed by Roberto Carlos against France during the confederation cup (held one year before the World Cup of 98).

The goalkeeper of France was Fabian Barthez. At that moment in time he was perhaps the best keeper in the world, along with Italy's Gianluigi Buffon of course! Anyway, Barthez aligned his wall perfectly and covered the dangerous angles beautifully. This forced Robert Carlos to attempt to shoot the ball around the wall.

Of course, no one had expected this, and with a little luck Carlos achieved what was probably the most spectacular free kick goal ever scored during a game.

My point is this; even when you cover all possible angles, there will always be a probability that a player will get the shot of his life and beat you, just like Roberto Carlos did! But under normal circumstances, if you get your act together well, then the odds are usually in your favor.

17 HANDLING CROSSED BALLS

It's crucial as a goalie that you know how to handle crossed balls. You only have to make one mistake in this area and you potentially give the opponents an ideal chance to kick the ball into an empty goal.

This is also one of the most common situations where amateurs fail. This is not because they're not good enough, in most cases, but more to do with them simply not knowing how to handle these situations properly.

I've seen this occur so many times, yet these keepers never seem to learn from their mistakes, which is why I've decided to include this chapter.

From what I've learned there are three basic rules to follow. Understand these and you will avoid facing the same destiny as so many other amateur goalies.

You might read these rules and think that they are just good common sense, and you'd be right. However, you would be truly amazed at just how many keepers never actually put any effort into applying them.

OK, I'm sure you are keen to find out what these rules are about, so let's start with most important one!

The number one rule for handling crossed balls – in my opinion – is to be 100% certain as to whether you should jump for the ball or remain on the ground. There is absolutely no room for doubting here because you can't afford making the wrong decision.

Inexperienced keepers often leap for crossed balls just for the sake of it, and that's despite the fact they know handling the ball safely is going to be really hard. Instead of helping the team, they end up causing a real mess by trying to grip the ball.

If there is an element of doubt in your mind, then you should not go for the ball. Instead, keep yourself on the goal line and wait for it to come to you. You have a better chance of saving the ball this way, compared to just jumping and hoping for the best.

The second rule is to make all players understand that you are the sheriff in town. In this case, that means you are the one who makes the decisions in the 18 yard box. Professional keepers are great at doing this and they are not afraid to manage their team.

You must really come across with authority and confidence here. Believe me, being firm will work wonders for handling crossed balls. Don't let anyone stand in your way when you are going for the ball. If they do, make sure they know who is in charge and get them to move quickly by acting with authority and conviction.

The third and final rule for handling crossed balls is to shout out your name when moving towards it. This will keep your defenders in the loop and help them to remain calm. Basically, what you are doing here is letting them know you are prepared for the ball and already on your way to take care of it so that they don't have to.

Shouting out your name will also go some way towards keeping most of your opponents at bay. They will usually think twice before trying to reach a ball that the goalie is preparing to catch.

If you decide to just jump without notifying your teammates, then they will have no clue that you are trying to handle the crossed ball. This could result in either a collision – where the outcome is that you drop the ball – or worse still you might cause serious injuries to yourself and others!

By following these three rules you will be able to eliminate a lot of the risk and dangers associated with handling crossed balls.

As mentioned in rule number two, you must always demonstrate authority and determination whenever the ball enters the 18 yard box.

18 FAST REFLEXES

Every goalkeeper dreams of having superfast, smooth reflexes.

In reality though, only few reach this level of skill because they are either not prepared to put the time and energy in that's needed to improve their current reflexes, or they are unwilling to try other methods.

As you have reached chapter 18 of this book, then I assume you are serious about your goalkeeping career and therefore willing to put in the work necessary for improving your reflexes.

The good news is that there's a way to enhance your reflex development, but you have to really want it if this is going to work.

However, you will be disappointed if you think you are going to be able to enhance your reflexes without hard work.

But providing you are willing to put in the effort, you will be pleased to know that there's a method that can help to fast track the development of your reflexes. Let us now look at this approach in some detail.

What I suggest you to do is start playing handball (a game in which the ball is hit with the hand in a walled court) and combine it with your indoor season. You are probably thinking what has handball actually got to do with soccer? Well, not much at all to be honest, but it is an ideal way for improving your reflexes as goalkeeper. Let me explain why.

By playing handball you have to save a lot of shots that are fired towards you from less than three yards. Practice at this and it's guaranteed to help develop your reflexes.

In case you're not convinced, I will now tell you something that'll help to change your mind.

Keep reading and you will soon realize that this is a powerful approach for improving your reflexes and consequently moving your game up to new level.

OK, so did you know that one of the best goalkeepers of all time played handball before he become professional? It's true. The goalie I am talking about is the Manchester United legend Peter Schmeichel.

Schmeichel has won countless trophies in his time. Some of the greatest are: Champions League, Premier League, and UEFA Euro Championship.

However, he has pointed out in several interviews that if he hadn't played handball in combination with soccer then he would never have reached his level of play. Never!

If that doesn't convince anyone that playing handball is a great way to improve reflexes and overall game, then nothing will.

The other great thing about handball is that it's played during the winter months. This means you can easily combine it with your indoor playing.

Work at this for a while and you will soon get to see how much your reflexes actually improve once you get out onto the regular field. Like anything else, the harder you work at this, the more you will benefit from it.

19 BEING TALL DOESN'T EQUAL SUCCESS

There is something of a myth among inexperienced and amateur keepers. That is, they are certain that you need to be extremely tall in order to become a highly successful goalie. I've actually seen wannabe goalkeepers give up their entire career just because they convinced themselves they were too short to succeed.

I can tell you now that nothing could be further from the truth, and don't let anyone or anything convince you otherwise.

This "tall" talk is nothing but a myth. Being tall doesn't guarantee success as a goalie any more than having long fingers ensures you'll be a great pianist

Obviously height can give some advantage over shorter goalkeepers, but being tall is not the same as being talented. You can be extremely short yet still be a world class goalkeeper and play in the biggest of competitions like the World Cup if you have the talent.

To illustrate this, let's look at one of the best Mexican goalkeepers of all time.

This guy was a highly successful goalie during his entire soccer career. He played at a time when there were several taller keepers around, and yet despite his shortness it was he, not them, who was the undisputable champion in goal.

So, who is this guy? His name is Jorge Francisco Campos Navarrete (nicknamed El Brody), a now retired Mexican footballer who played as a striker as well as a goalkeeper back in his day.

He had a really successful international career spanning from 1988 to 2004. He posed great reflexes that he combined with an incredible understanding for the game.

The most impressive thing about Campos, besides his great goalkeeping skills, was the fact that he was extremely short for a world class goalie, standing at only 5' 6". This was then, and still is now, well below the average height for soccer goalies. Today, a lot of professional keepers have an average height of around 6'3".

While he had some difficulties with crossed balls from time to time, he often combined these weaker sides with great resilience and an ability to read the game. He also posed incredible leaping skills and speed which undoubtedly contributed to his success.

He was also one of the top goalies during the World Cup 1994 which was held in the U.S.A. It was here that he got to show the whole world that you really don't have to be tall to be a highly successful goalkeeper.

The reason for using Jorge Luis Campos as an example is to show you that being under a certain height does not have to become your downfall.

Your goalie career is not doomed because of your height, but it could be ruined by a false conviction if you let myths and detractors influence you. Instead, become inspired by Campos and realize that only you can stop yourself from reaching the top, not your height.

20 IMPROVING CONFIDENCE

Having confidence is one of the fundamental requirements for performing consistently well and succeeding as a goalkeeper.

A lack of self-assurance will mean your performance on the field is going to be much less than what it could be.

The question here is how can you build your confidence level up, and furthermore, how long will it take to improve in this area?

Well, perhaps the main problem here is that goalkeeping is often a lonely job, and unless you stay mindful and energized of your responsibilities, it's easy to become disheartened. This is when self-doubt can creep in and knock your confidence for six.

One good strategy for improving your goalkeeping confidence is to stand in front of a mirror, look yourself in the eyes, and then say these words out loud with conviction: "From this moment on I will start believing in myself."

Repeat several times, or for about one minute, and make it a daily ritual, twice a day, morning and evening.

Remember, it is important to really believe what you are saying.

Also emphasize the point that if you are not working on your own self-confidence, then no one else can do it for you.

Many years ago I had this one friend who was a very skillful goalkeeper but his confidence was really poor.

He could do amazing saves during practice, when the pressure was off, but as soon as we played in a competition he would often fail miserably and make silly mistakes; mistakes he would never have made during training.

One day I decided to ask him why he was playing so well during practice, yet performing so poorly during real games. He simply said that he lacked the confidence to perform the same way in actual competition.

I then suggested the mirror method to him. I proposed that he stands in front of a mirror each day, twice a day, once when he wakes up, and again before he goes to bed, and says out loud that he has confidence in himself and his game during competition.

I explained that these chants, for want of a better word, are known as positive affirmations, and it has been proven time and time again that this approach really does work at helping to build a person's confidence.

At first he was hesitant about this, and I could see by the expression on his face that he thought it was a bit daft.

However, I just said that he has absolutely nothing to lose by giving it a go, and how anyone can afford to take a couple of minutes out of their day, no matter how busy they are.

Furthermore, I pointed out that this is something that can be done in total privacy, so it's not as if he needs to feel foolish in front of others.

Anyhow, he reluctantly decided to give it a go, and guess what? I immediately saw an improvement in his performance during the very next game. And after one month, well, he was a completely different goalkeeper.

He thanked me sincerely for helping him improve his performance, and said he would never have been able to do it without me.

I explained that I did little more than pass on an exercise for improving self-confidence, and that it was he, not I, who did the work. I merely gave him the tools for which to use.

What you should learn from this chapter is the fact that YOU must believe in your own skills and abilities. If you don't, then nor will anyone else!

Confidence will have a huge impact on your overall performance, which is why you need to work on improving and maintaining it – always!

21 CHOOSING THE RIGHT GLOVES

The most important part of your kit are the gloves. They decide how well you are able to grip the ball, and "grip" is everything to a goalie.

It can mean the difference between a magnificent save and a good try. Poor gloves can really ruin your performance, so it's important to pay attention to this and explore your options.

I am sure you have already faced the dilemma of purchasing a new pair of gloves.

There are countless brands out there, all using different materials, of varying fits and sizes, and extremes in price, ranging from just a few dollars to a couple of hundred. So just how can you know what to buy and what to avoid?

Let's start by looking at the size of the gloves. Sizes vary from 4 (youth) to 12 (adults).

This is just a general guide so you must always try your gloves on before you buy them, just as you would do a new pair of boots.

You will often find expensive gloves considerably cheaper on the internet, but it's never a good idea to make a blind purchase.

What I suggest is that you visit your local sports store first and tryout the different gloves available. Once you find something suitable, make a note of the price, name, and brand, and then search for the same items online.

There's a very good chance you will find the same gloves at least 30% cheaper on the net compared to the prices at your local store. If you are serious about your goalkeeping, then you should opt for the more expensive gloves as they will be of higher overall quality.

It's also important that your gloves fit you perfectly. What this means is that they should feel snug but not too tight, and they should definitely not be too loose. If they're too big then you will not be able to maintain your grip on the ball properly.

During my early twenties I played with a goalkeeper who was really good at saving shots but lousy at keeping his grip on the ball when catching it, especially with high powered shots. Clearly this was frustrating as it meant there were times when he'd mess things up for the team.

One day after a match, when we were in the locker room, I compared my hands with his. I could see that they were pretty equal in size and so and I asked if I could try on his gloves.

The moment I put them on it became obvious that his inability to grip the ball was because his gloves where way too big.

He said that he'd never really given this any thought and was not totally convinced that there was anything wrong with the size of his gloves, so we approached the coach.

The coach confirmed that his gloves were far too large for his hands. Later that day he took him to the local sports store where he got to find out what right-sized gloves actually felt like.

As you have probably guessed, he purchased a new pair there and then and his days of dropping the ball were to become a thing of the past.

The lesson you should draw from this chapter is to understand what a pair of correctly fitting gloves actually feels like.

Whatever you do, always make sure you try them on before making a purchase. Go for the best quality that you can afford.

If you are not sure how to determine "quality" then just get a pair that costs more. Seriously, when it comes to goalkeeper gloves, you really do get what you pay for.

22. IMPROVING YOUR GOALKEEPING INTELLECT

I just want to start by saying that goalkeeping intelligence has nothing to do with your personal intellect.

In fact, you can be really smart yet still lack the intelligence or mindset of a sharp goalie. Don't worry though as this is something that can also be acquired.

However, developing your 'goalie intelligence' is not the easiest of skills to improve. This is because you generally need to have a lot of practical experience on the soccer field in order to develop the right mindset.

Fortunately though, I do have something of a shortcut that will help you develop your mind to that of a more astute and experienced goalkeeper.

OK, so let's now take a look at just how to achieve this. The way to improve your goalie intelligence is to watch as much soccer as possible on TV, the internet, and in the real world.

While this might seem obvious, there is an important aspect that will decide how much you gain from this method; so what is it?

It's called "study mode." This simply means that you do not get emotionally involved in the game at all. Instead, you are studying it from a neutral perspective.

The difference here is that you review the game and its players, as opposed to sitting back and watching the match.

The idea is that you look carefully for new things that can help improve your own performance on the field.

For example, you might study a highly successful goalkeeper who plays for your favorite team.

However, as you want to improve your skills and not get emotionally involved in the game, you should only monitor what he is doing.

To help get you in the right mode I have outlined a few pointers below. Look at these carefully as they will help you understand how to analyze a goalkeeper's performance while at the same time work at improving your own goalkeeping intelligence:

- How fast does he reinstate the game after saving a shot?
- In which type of situations does he clear the ball away?
- In which situations does he receive the ball without clearing it away?
- What actions does he use too coordinate his teammates in defense?
- Does he punch the ball more often than catch it?
- Is he communicating constantly or just at certain times?
- In what situations does he sacrifice himself for the team?

These points should give you a good idea of the types of things to monitor in order to improve your intelligence as goalkeeper.

There are obviously many more observations you can make, but the ones above will give you a good place to start as you prepare a priority list of your own.

If you can, I recommend you watch as many games as possible in real world. The reason for this is because on TV the goalie is usually out of shot until the ball is near or inside the 18 yard box.

Not having the keeper within sight for the entire match means you will miss other important details that could help improve your intelligence on the field.

23 THE IMPORTANCE OF DETERMINATION & COMMITMENT

Determination and commitment is what creates real champions. These qualities are necessary for anyone who wants to become professional. Talent is also obviously important, but it's not enough on its own.

So what does it actually mean to be determined and committed? Well, one clear example will be to put soccer above all else.

You will not have to grapple with your mind or toss a coin to decide whether your hobby activities like playing games, watching movies, or going to disco, take precedence over your soccer.

Nothing, and I mean nothing, will come between you and your commitment to the game.

In order to get an edge over the competition you may have to sacrifice your hobby activities, or at least cut down on the time you give to them so that you can focus completely on developing your goalkeeping skills.

This is not something that you can do halfheartedly if you expect to become a highly successful goalkeeper.

Think of this as similar to preparing for school examinations.

Students who want to do well will most likely sacrifice all their hobby activities as they totally focus their minds on the tests ahead.

In other words, they are determined and committed to pass and nothing or nobody will stand in their way.

However, there is a distinct difference between the scenario above and what we're looking at here.

A school examination is something that will come and go in a relatively short space of time.

What's more is that the closer a student gets to the tests the more commitment and determination they will need. Then, once the exams are over, they can happily return to their leisure activities.

But for you as a goalkeeper in the making, your commitment and dedication is unrelenting and becomes a part of who you are.

For you, this is a lifestyle change and not something you do for a short period of time.

If you have ever watched or read an interview with a professional and highly successful goalkeeper, then you will probably have picked up on that one question which always gets asked at personal interviews:

How were you able to reach the top of your game and become the success that you are?

I have observed hundreds such interviews throughout my soccer career, and the one common thing I've noticed is that these goalkeepers always focus on the importance of dedication and commitment.

They all say the same thing and the answers are so predictable: "The only reason I got so good at my game was because I put it above all else, no matter what!"

You see, when someone is highly determined and committed, then willpower is not needed most of the time.

When soccer becomes something you live and breathe for, then you don't need to fight with your mind to get up and get practicing; it's something you want to do simply because you love it.

To summarize this chapter: you too must become fired up and excited about your development. If your ambition is to become more than just another Joe Average goalie, then determination and commitment has to be hardwired into you psyche.

The journey will be tough at times, but so long as you are unwavering in your dedication then you goals will materialize.

24 NUTRITION = GAS

I cannot emphasizes the importance of nutrition strongly enough. Good nourishment is fundamental to your performance.

Hopefully, after reading this chapter you will also recognize the importance of healthy eating and note how it energizes both the body and mind.

Anything that requires power to operate needs fuel of some sort. A car, for example, needs gas, and without it there is no energy to drive the vehicle. Or, put substandard fuel in the tank and it doesn't run as well as it should do.

We humans also need fuel, and like the car, we can't perform without it. Or, if put substandard fuel into our bodies, aka junk food, and we become sluggish and function with limited capacity

Athletes need to understand what kind of food they should be eating. As a goalkeeper, one type of food you want to keep on the menu is quality carbohydrates like pasta.

One of my favorite meals is meat sauce combined with pasta. Here in Sweden, spaghetti Bolognese is the most popular type of meal for soccer players.

Try to eat some fat with your protein as well because it's necessary you maintain a balanced diet. A general rule is to consume about 40% carbohydrates, 30% fat and 30% protein. This is the ultimate soccer diet and it's going to do wonders for your performance.

What you must also do is avoid all fast foods as it doesn't contain the necessary nutrition required to run your engine properly.

My recommendation is to forget about its existence altogether if you can. Apart from lacking in nourishment, it's also harmful to health, especially when consumed regularly.

I'm proud to say that I have not touched any kind of fast food, convenience food, junk food, call it what you will, for a good many years now, and I feel as fit as a butcher's dog because of it.

How did I wean off fast food? I just woke up one morning and decided there was no point in putting anything into my body that did nothing to enhance my performance on the soccer field. Okay, so it was a bit tough to begin with, but it wasn't too long before I broke the habit.

If you are serious about becoming healthy and maintaining your fitness levels, then my advice is to forget about fast foods and focus on boosting your energy levels and overall performance by eating well.

You probably remember what we discussed previously about sacrificing certain things in order to reach your goals. Well, poor diet is one of those things you must get rid of if you truly want to achieve your dream of becoming a professional or semi-professional goalkeeper.

To summarize this chapter: Don't look to amateur goalies for guidance on healthy eating. The majority of recreational goalkeepers don't look too much into the importance of proper nutrition because they, unlike you, are not preoccupied about becoming professional, or playing in more serious competitions.

Once you appreciate and actually get to experience the difference that a well-balanced and nutritious diet can provide for you, I am pretty certain you will never want to return to any old, unhealthy eating habits that you may have acquired over the years.

25 THE PURPOSE OF PRACTICE

Do you ever go to practice sessions without any clear objective about what area of your game you would like to work on?

Most amateurs simply perform whatever drills are instructed by the coach - without question! If you can identify with that, then it's time to re-think the purpose and potential of the practice session.

Most amateur teams have no extra money to spend on hiring an additional coach who can work on specific drills suited to the keeper. This lack of attention towards goalies is actually quite unfair because the goalkeeper is often left to work his own program.

OK, so things are the way they are, and if the keeper has to take responsibility for most of his own training, then that's what he must do.

This means you will have to be a bit more disciplined than the rest of the team, as they get most of their guidance from the coach, whereas you will have to fend for yourself.

Therefore, before each practice session I recommend you sit down for at least 30 minutes and go through those areas of your game you would like to improve.

One example might be that you could do with improving your grip.

So instead of participating in general drills that are more tailored to the field players, you would ask the coach to let you practice on your grip as an alternative.

There are many goalie-specific drills you can work on alone, and it's your responsibility as a keeper to research them and shape your own program.

The mistake most amateur keepers make is that they think someone will take care of their training needs, but this is one luxury that won't be available until later in your career.

For as long as you are an amateur, you will need to spend a lot of time taking responsibility for improving your own performance.

This means you will often have to detach yourself from the regular training sessions and do your own thing.

Let's imagine, for instance, that you have a training session later this evening and that you have just arrived home.

You would first eat a proper meal (see chapter 24.), then perhaps lie down on the bed or stretch out on the sofa for a while to relax a bit before heading out.

This is a good time to start reflecting over the purpose of your forthcoming practice.

It's a good idea to have a notebook handy so that you can jot down any thoughts you have for the upcoming practice.

To give you some idea on the kinds of things you might write, I have made a shortlist of questions that should help get you thinking. These are:

- How should I organize the practice so as to get the most out of it?
- What skills should I focus on improving today?
- Is there any skill(s) that needs to be worked on as a priority?

- What specific drills can I use to improve this/these skill(s)?
- Can I perform these drills alone or do I need assistance?

The sample questions above are just guidelines, but they should give you a good idea of the kind of things you need to be asking yourself.

This is a much more efficient approach for a goalie to get himself well-organized compared to just flowing with the field players at each and every practice.

In all the teams I have played at amateur level, the keeper was expected to practice with the rest of the team or on his own, and without any real direction from the coach.

This is why you need to pay attention to the solo strategy. Attending practice without any real purpose of what areas you want to improve on will do nothing to help you develop as a goalie.

26 PASSES INTO FREE SPACE

Passes into free spaces are one of the goalie's worst nightmares, not least because he has to judge whether there is enough time to clear the ball away before the opponent gets to it.

This requires quick thinking and a good knowledge of the game as a whole. The only way to avoid messing up is to be absolutely sure that you can reach the ball before the opponent.

This is why you need to monitor the attacking players and study their skills, especially speed as it will be important in these kinds of duels.

As you can see, as the keeper you are actually part of the defense. This comes with a lot of responsibility because you have to clear away any passes that are played into free space.

Quite often, the center fullbacks will not be able to compete with a right-turned attacker as he will already have few yards advantage. In scenarios like this you are the last outpost of defense. That means if you fail to clear the ball away, then there's a very good chance you will give the opponents an opportunity to roll the ball into the goal.

The problem with this skill is that you need to have enough confidence in your ability to leave the 18 yard box.

Most amateur keepers are not aware of the importance of this skill. Once the ball has passed through the defense line, the keeper doesn't usually get a chance to save the day.

And once the opponents reach the 18 yard box, they will have a free road towards the goal, and that means saving the ball will be really tough, if not impossible.

Another danger with failing to reach the ball in time is that you can easily earn a red card and get sent off the field if you're not careful.

You need to ask yourself whether trying to clear the ball away is worth risking a red card for, especially if the odds are against you.

The moment you get out of the 18 yard box there is no time for hesitation. The decision has been made, so you must fulfill your attempt and try to clear the ball away no matter what!

Think of this like trying to save a penalty, in that once you dive in a certain direction there is no opportunity for changing your mind.

One way of improving your ability with this is to practice with a couple of teammates. Simply get one co-player to pass the ball into free space while the other is running after it.

This is a good way to get a feel for the situation and to sharpen up you confidence. You will also develop your gut feeling on whether you'd be able to reach the ball in time or not.

Try doing this from several parts of the field with different types of passes such as long, short, high, and so on.

After about twenty exercises, take a break and evaluate how many times you were able to clear the ball without fouling your teammate.

If you have fouled your teammate just once or twice per twenty repetitions then you have done well and are less likely to earn a red card in real games.

However, if you caused a foul for every second or third attempt, then you need to practice more on improving this skill.

To summarize this chapter: In order to be mastered well I would say that this is one skill which requires a lot of experience and understanding of the game. It is therefore important to have patience and to keep working on it.

Don't worry too much if your attempts earn you a red card from time to time. Remember, the best way to learn something new is from your own mistakes.

27 MISJUDGING THE PATH

Have you ever seen a goal scored where the keeper looked like a complete amateur despite actually being a true professional?

A typical situation where this type of goals occurs is when the keeper misjudges the path.

This is especially true when the ball is fired from a long range kick (more than 50 yards). Such shots can lure the keeper into a false sense of safety, often thinking he has total control of the situation.

However, the story I'm about to tell you shows how it's never wise to assume anything in the game of soccer.

My strongest memory pertaining to this topic is a game from several years ago.

We had two competitors who were hot on our heels at the time, which meant we had to win all of our remaining games if we were to triumph.

As you might expect, this put a lot of pressure on both the players and our coach.

In the first half of the match we had a 1-0 lead and were pretty much in control of the game.

However, the opponents scored from a corner kick at the beginning of the second half and the panic started to spread among the team. Fortunately for us, our keeper was doing very well managed to keep us in the game.

When there was about ten minutes of the game remaining, our opponents got a free kick on their half of the field.

One of their players crossed the ball towards our goal as he attempted to reach the striker.

However, the ball got a really high path and we all just stood as we watched it soar through the air. None of us thought for a second that our keeper was about to make a terrible mistake and let the ball pass into the goal.

But he did!

The referee blew his whistle and the opponents celebrated frantically. We had just witnessed one of soccer's unpredictable events!

Our keeper simply failed to predict the path of the ball and it landed just under the crossbar. This was unbelievable considering that he was standing on the goal line. His explanation later was that he thought the ball would fly over the crossbar.

What happened was that a strong gust of wind changed the path of the ball as it entered the 18 yard box, thus driving it under the crossbar.

We lost that game and the team was really disappointed because it shouldn't have ended like this.

We just could not understand how a competent keeper could allow a goal in from a cross of some 60 yards. This was not only a lost game, but a humiliation too!

But that was then and this is now. Today when I think about it, I can understand better how it happened.

The goalkeeper did have total control of the situation as the ball approached him, and he was right to think it would pass over the crossbar on its current path.

But that unpredictable gust of wind at the very last minute could not have been anticipated – obviously - but where the keeper went wrong was that he wasn't prepared for the unexpected, and in soccer, complacency is never a good idea.

What I would you like to learn from this account is that you should always pay attention to the path of the ball as it travels toward the goal, and never assume its final destination.

If you don't heed this warning, then there will always be a risk of messing up, just like our goalkeeper did.

28 MAKE IT GAME LIKE

The secret to improving your goalkeeping skills as quickly as possible is to make every practice session game like.

While it might sound easy, it's actually quite difficult to adopt this mindset if you are not used to it.

It could take you quite a while to get completely comfortable with making practice game-like. I'm telling you this from my own experience.

I've seen a lot of goalkeepers who had a hard time adapting themselves to actually practice in this way.

Amateur goalkeepers tend to flow with the pack and only occasionally put in the extra effort to improve their skills.

During practice, they often have short peaks where they play like they do in actual games. However, the rest of the time they are just trying to play with as little effort as possible.

Because you are reading this book, it is my hope that you will not make the same mistake, or if you do currently slack-off during practice then you will now break the habit.

After all, your primary aim is to become the best goalkeeper that you can possibly be, and that means slacking is not an option.

So just how do you actually get into game mode during training? This is something that's a lot simpler than you might think.

All you have to do is get into the same mindset during practice as you would do during real games. I said it was simple, but I didn't say it was easy!

The important thing in the beginning is to constantly remind yourself to take practice seriously, even if others around you are not.

Fake this mental approach until you make it if you have to, but whatever you do, don't let your guard down. Eventually, treating practice sessions as serious as you would do a real competition will become natural behavior to you.

Try to look at this as having a coach who constantly screams at you to perform better. In this case however, you are responsible for creating this coach in your mind because you can't expect the real one to do this. He will likely have at least 20 other players to coordinate.

Carry this mindset with you at all times, even when you are playing backyard soccer with your mates. Having a kick-around with friends is another time where amateur goalkeepers tend to fall into slothful ways.

But from now on, you should treat every opportunity as if you were playing in a serious competition. Do this, and you will see your performance skyrocket.

If I were you I would create a hard and fixed rule for myself in that each time I played soccer I would make it game-like, no matter what the circumstance or attitude of the other players! It shouldn't matter whether it's a cup final or just a game in the backyard.

Your goal here is to become hardwired into treating each and every opportunity as one to improve your skills.

To summarize this chapter: It's important to be mindful of the fact that what you put into your game is what you will get out.

In other words, the more effort, focus and dedication that you devote to improving your skills by making every opportunity "game like," the further you will go in your soccer career.

29 THE FREE KICK WALL

Whether you will save a free kick or not often depends on how well you have positioned your wall of defense and the type of players standing in it. In general, the taller your teammates are, the more chance there is of the ball getting caught in the wall.

It's also important for you to coordinate the wall so that your teammates are covering all possible gaps from where opponents could score.

You need to pay close attention to where the wall is standing, and if necessary, move it around so that the defenders are blocking the path of the ball as best as possible.

You should be aware that very few players actually have the skill to bend the ball over the wall perfectly and score.

This means that most of the opponents you play against will usually just take the shot and hope some scoring opportunity comes out of it.

This is why it's important to pay close attention to your wall. Make sure it's synchronized and positioned exactly where you want it to be.

There are a few other points (see below) that you should pay attention to which can also decide the outcome of a free kick.

These points may seem obvious, but you would be astonished at how many keepers fail to utilize them correctly in their game.

Remain mindful of these in your own game and implement them carefully.

- Make sure your wall doesn't jump just before the opponent releases the shot. If they do, he could easily shoot low leaving you with very little chance to save the ball.

- You should have one player turned against you who operates as coordinator and puts your direction into practice by moving the wall either to the left or the right.

- Does the coordinator know that he is supposed to move the wall slightly towards the shooter if he gets the chance? Although this is not normally allowed, if the referee doesn't see it, then it's worth a try.

- Inspect the wall for possible gaps and make sure it's as compact as possible so as to prevent the opponent from shooting through it.

As previously mentioned, ALL of these points are important as they can determine the outcome of a free kick.

Remember that you only get one chance to prevent the opponent from scoring, so work smart when arranging your wall of defense.

Also worth a mention is that shooters might pass the ball to the sideline.

They may even roll it backwards to another player who would then be the one to actually fire the shot.

In cases such as these, you would need to slightly adjust your position while the wall should maintain where it is.

There is always a chance that an opponent will become lucky and get the shot of his life; the one that evades any defense you have in place.

If this happens, then there will be very little you can do to save the day.

However, don't assume the worse. Make sure you place your main focus purely on stopping any attempts to score.

Think about what you can do to succeed and not what might happen if you fail (see chapter 37 on how to quickly remove thoughts of failure).

30 SAVING A PENALTY KICK

The best thing about penalties is that you have a mental advantage over your opponent. It is he who has the greatest pressure on him.

Your job as goalkeeper is to try and figure out where he is likely to shoot and then dive in that direction when the time comes.

It's important to know that if you fail to save a penalty then no one is going to blame you for it.

While on the other hand, if you happen to save the shot, then you could easily become the hero of the match and lead your team to victory.

In short, you have a lot to win, but very little to lose. In these situations, being a goalie can be a real joy.

Before you lose yourself and start fantasying about saving these penalties, let me pass you some really effective tips that will increase your chances of stopping a penalty shot.

The more of these you can successfully interpret and turn to your advantage, the more you will increase your chance of making a successful save.

- Where is the opponent focusing his look? Does he specifically peer more in the direction of the goal, or is he maintaining a neutral focus and making it hard to read where he actually plans to shoot?
- Is the one taking the penalty using some specific body language before the kick? Some players like to perform specific rituals which could reveal where they plan to shoot.
- Can you get eye contact with the opponent? One easy way to get visual contact with him is to walk over, and then look him right in the eyes as you pass the ball and wish him good luck.
- Which direction is his supporting foot pointing. Quite often, the direction of the supporting foot reveals the direction he plans to fire the shot, thus giving you a chance to get there in time.
- Lure the opponent by pretending to go in one direction but then dive in the other. The idea is to have the opponent shoot in the opposing direction.
- Is he right or left footed? Generally, right-footed players often shoot to the left, whereas left-footed players prefer to shoot to the right.
- Dance and or run from side to side while waving your arms around.

As you can see there are numerous things you can do and consider before the opponent has even fired the shot at your goal.

The more of these you incorporate in your style of play, the more overall success you will have with saving penalties.

Now if you think about those penalty kicks you have witnessed during professional games, you can probably recall how the keeper adapted several of the above points prior to the shot being taken.

Something that's worth a mention here is that occasionally a referee might consider your actions and motives unfair and give you a yellow card.

In my experience though, you shouldn't need to worry about this happening provided you don't overdo the suggestions above and use good common sense.

31 SAVING CORNERS

For an inexperienced keeper, knowing whether to go for the ball during a corner or remain on the goal line and wait for it to come to you can be a really tough decision.

A lot of goalies fail in this area simply because they haven't done their homework. Because you've found my book and come this far, you will not be making the same mistakes.

Once the corner kick is released you need to decide whether you should jump for the ball or not.

A general rule is to try and predict whether it's coming into your six yard box. If you are certain that it's coming this way then you should go for it without hesitation.

It is really important to understand that once you have made your decision to go for the ball there is no turning back.

If you hesitate or change your mind at the very last minute, then there's a real chance that things could go horribly wrong.

Any indecisiveness will most likely result in giving the opponents an opportunity to score.

I have listed other important details below that need to be heeded during a corner kick. To leave any of these out will likely have a negative impact on your performance, and also decrease the chance of saving a header.

- Make sure you have one player at each post, covering the angles that you would find hard to reach from your position.
- Focus on coordinating your teammates quickly so that each of them is covering one opponent.
- Get the tallest and strongest team players to mark opponents who you think or know to be skillful at headers.
- It is important to have your teammates understand that they must follow the opponent they are marking at least until the ball has been cleared away.
- Always shout your name out loud when going up for the ball. Failure to do so may result in you punching one of your teammates in the head as he himself tries to clear it.

The great thing about being a goalkeeper is that during corner kicks the referee will usually side with you.

This means that if an opponent tries to block you from getting the ball, the ref will often give you a free kick.

Obviously you can't rely on this and expect to get awarded a free kick with every corner. My reason for mentioning this is to make you aware of how things work.

This in turn should make you less cautious when trying to reach for the ball, especially with those more ambitious leaps.

To summarize this chapter: I want to reemphasize the fact that inside the 18 yard box you are the boss.

This is your domain and it is your responsibility to take advantage of it and make things happen in your favor.

Never ever allow your opponents to become the dominant force inside this area.

If you do, then your chances of saving a header will be greatly diminished.

Furthermore, any lack of authority from you within the 18 yard box will make you look really weak from the side, and your influence as a goalkeeper will be questioned.

32 THE IMPORTANCE OF A GOAL KICK

The goal kick is not crucial for being a great keeper, but it can do wonders for your team if you are able to pull it off with power and accuracy.

I've often found that a lot of goalies are unable to kick the ball very far which limits the chances of it reaching the attacking players and creating scoring opportunities.

Quite often, you will see other players help the goalkeeper perform the goal kick, which is an easy solution to the problem.

However, if you want to play higher than amateur soccer then you will need to become better than just average at this yourself.

A professional goalkeeper should be able to take a goal-kick and perform it with perfection.

But apart from that, it looks really unprofessional having a fellow teammate taking a goal kick for the goalie, unless of course he has an injury that prevents him from performing it.

There are few pointers that can help you master the art of the goal kick. I have listed the ones below that I think you should focus on the most:

- You must pull your kicking leg back as much as possible (just like a catapult) in order to generate sufficient power for striking the ball hard.
- The ankle of your kicking foot should be firmly locked and you should try to perform the kick pretty much with a spade-like action.
- Try to keep the knee of your supporting leg slightly bent so as to maintain good balance during the kick.
- Lean your body slightly backwards as this will help you get height on the ball. The more you lean backwards, the more height you will add to the ball as it soars through the air.
- Make sure to follow-through as you strike the ball. Following through will create a smoother, more controlled action as you release the kick, and therefore improve the accuracy of it.

Although I agree that these points can seem a little overwhelming at first, I can assure you that once the basics have been learned, it will only be a matter of time before you master this skill and perform it on autopilot.

Depending on your talent and current ability, you might only need few practices before you get to move your goal-kicking skills up to the next level.

I would say that most amateur goalkeepers would generally need a few months of regular practice (3-4 times per week) before they are able to perform a goal kick with far greater accuracy and increased power.

To summarize this chapter: I want to stress the importance on how a properly executed goal kick can be really efficient for creating scoring opportunities, especially if your strikers are faster on their feet than the opponents defense line.

33 LIVING LIKE A PROFESSIONAL

Do you genuinely want to become a professional goalkeeper yet live your life as an amateur?

If yes, then you had better re-think your strategy.

If you want to make the big teams then you will need to start living and breathing as if you were already a true pro.

David James, the former national team keeper of England, said that you should treat your body like a car enthusiast looks after his Rolls Royce.

What he meant by this is that you need to constantly keep your body in pristine condition so as to maintain its shine and performance.

So what does it actually mean in practice, and where should you start?

Well, the best place to begin is by paying close attention to what you eat. The importance of nutrition cannot be emphasized strongly enough.

Seriously, consuming the wrong types of food can have a huge negative impact in more ways than one.

Sitting or slouching on the sofa watching late evening television the night before a game is not a smart thing to do.

It's also a bad idea to go out partying until well after midnight.

Getting quality kip is not just about the number of hours you spend in slumber (although a good eight hours is recommended), but it also includes the quality of that sleep.

Getting peaceful, uninterrupted sleep is without doubt one of the most important variables for improving overall brain function, longevity, and performance in all aspects of life.

Be careful not to overexert yourself too. In my experience, one of the fastest ways to mess with your performance is to practice too much.

There's a big difference between lots of practice and too much practice, or to put it another way, being enthusiastic and overly enthusiastic.

You may well be as keen as mustard, but overexerting yourself prior to a game can sap you of that much needed energy on match day, thus making it difficult to reload your batteries.

My advice is to rest at least one day before a game.

There are a number of other, smaller details that contribute to the lifestyle of a professional keeper.

Below is a complete list of things which I consider to be the most important:

- Proper hydration: be sure to drink at least 2 liters of water on game day.
- Listening to your favorite music: this is a great way to charge yourself with positive energy.
- Focus completely on your tasks: it means be mindful of the role you have to play – specifically - and don't get caught up with reflecting over the nitty-gritty details of the entire game.
- Keep yourself relaxed: it's important to learn how to relax completely, while at the same time maintaining good concentration and focus.

- Visualize success: this can be achieved by leaving out negative thoughts and focusing only on positive outcome and performance.
- Emit personal problems: in other words, don't let whatever private issues you have dominate your thoughts and take up all your time. Replace them by focusing solely only on your game, especially during practice and on match days.
- Warm up properly: this means correct and gentle stretching alternated with walking/jogging for at least 15 minutes. By doing this you achieve proper blood flow to the areas that will be used during play, thus reducing the risk of unnecessary injury.

All of these points contribute towards the professional lifestyle. As you can see, there will be some sacrifices that have to be made.

If you want to have the same regime as a true pro, it means that you will have a huge personal responsibility for making things work.

This is no easy feat, which is why so many soccer wannabes are unable to become professional. As mentioned previously, talent alone is not enough to make it big in this business.

You have to remember one important thing as you strive to develop and maintain your soccer career, which is: what you put in is what you will get back.

That's it in a nutshell!

You can't expect to reach the top without living like a champ, and that means sacrificing anything that could hinder your progress.

34 WORKING ON YOUR BASICS

In order to develop your goalkeeping abilities you will need to constantly learn new skills and incorporate them into your own game. However, what most goalies tend to forget is to work on the basic skills, i.e. the ones you could do in your sleep.

The danger with forgetting the importance of the basics is that you can become nonchalant and take them for granted.

As you know, nothing in soccer comes for free, so in order to maintain and develop all your skills you will have to work on the basics as well as the more advanced ones.

When I was just 15 years old, we were facing the second placed team in our competition. Although we occupied the number one spot, these guys were still hot on our heels with only two points behind.

The goalkeeper of our team, who also happened to be my class mate, was really skillful and I admired his talents.

The only problem he had was that he could become too laidback from time to time. When he got into "detached mode" he would really mess up the most basic of things.

During one of our games he was about to catch a straightforward long-range shot, yet his complacency saw him drop that ball.

Not unexpectedly, the opponents who were luring in front of the goal then managed to score as a result of his blunder.

If you think that's bad enough, it gets worse! In our next game he made the exact same mistake again. And the game after that, he dropped yet another ball from what should have been a simple catch!

The coach at the time was the paternal father of our goalie, and he wasn't comfortable criticizing his own son in front of the other players, much to the dismay of the rest of the team.

I eventually decided to take this into my own hands seeing as we were friends. So as we were stretching one day during the warm up, I told him that I'd like to have as word if that was ok.

The rest of the team was looking at me somewhat confused. I could see from the looks on their faces that they had no idea what was about to come.

The coach allowed me to speak, so I just got on and said what needed to be said - but hadn't been!

"Jimmy (the goalie)? I think you need to start working on your catching skills. We can't continue like this with you making the same mistakes that you have been doing in recent games."

There was a deadly silence and I could sense that the other guys, including the Dad, were embarrassed for Jimmy, but these things needed to be said, so I continued while I was on a role.

"I also believe that you should stop being so nonchalant and start to more pay attention to the most basic skills of a goalie, and that is to "CATCH" the ball. You're a good goalie Jimmy, but you've let your game slip of late, and it's affecting us all."

I didn't know quite know what response to expect, and after a brief pause Jimmy stood up and said:

"Mirsad? You are absolutely right in what you say. I do need to start paying more attention during games. I also need to start working on my basic skills more instead of just jogging around during practice, killing time. And as much as I didn't like to be called "nonchalant," I know that I have been, and I would like to apologize to the team for letting you all down these past months."

Wow! I didn't envisage that. If anything, I was preparing for a heated debate, an argument even!

What Jimmy said was completely unexpected.

His response was mature, humble, and music to our ears.

From that practice on, Jimmy became a completely different goalkeeper.

He kept true to his word and never made simple mistakes ever again. We performed a lot better as a team too, all thanks to the changing attitude of a single player.

After the last match of the season, Jimmy approached me and said that the day I constructively criticized him in front of the team, was the day that he changed for the better.

On that note, we shook hands and then began to reflect on the highs and lows of the season.

To summarize this chapter: Jimmy came to realize that he needed to start working more on his "basic" skills. It was apparent to everyone but him (until his wakeup call) that he was letting them slip.

What you should learn from this is the fact that no ability remains the same unless you work at maintaining your skills; no matter how basic something might be, like catching a flying ball!

35 DISCOURAGEMENT & MISTAKES

Making mistakes during a match is an inevitable part of any game. It doesn't matter how hard you try to avoid blunders, sooner or later you will directly or indirectly mess up somewhere.

When it does happen, amateur keepers tend to take things very personally; something which obviously affects their performance negatively.

You must learn to avoid these feelings of guilt at all costs. When all said and done, once you've made a mistake that results in a goal for the opposition, you need to understand that it can't be undone. That's it!

There's no point or time for replaying the incident over in your mind; the goal has been scored and you need to just hold your head high and focus on the rest of the game.

The faster you can put a slip-up behind you and forget about it, the easier it will be for you to continue performing at pre-gaffe level and move on with the game.

With an attitude of "onwards and upwards" you will develop and strengthen your mental ability to accept a defeat for what it is, and that can only be a good thing for confidence building too.

Getting down about a mistake will not only negatively affect your performance, but that of the entire team too.

After all, soccer is a team sport, meaning they need you as much as you need them.

So the best strategy after a slip-up is to dust yourself off and prove your worth to yourself and the team by performing well for the remainder of the match.

If you study professional keepers, you will notice how they are able to quickly forget any mistakes they make and continue on with conviction and determination as if nothing had happened.

In my experience, the most effective way to get over a soccer blunder is to close the eyes for few seconds, take two or three deep breaths, and tell yourself that what is done can't be undone, and that the most important thing now is to press on with the game.

I know it sounds a bit cliché, but if you put enough thought into this mental strategy, then it can really work wonders for getting over a failure on the pitch. You see, the only effective way to get rid of a negative thought is to replace it with a positive one.

One of my old teammates, who also happened to be a fantastic goalkeeper when he was on form, had a lot of difficulty handling his mistakes.

He was a perfectionist through and through, which meant he placed tremendous pressure on himself to perform well at all times. Consequently, whenever he fell short of his own expectations, he would beat himself up.

Any time he made a mistake that allowed the opposition to score, you could visibly see how discouraged and disappointed he became with himself. Even on occasions where he'd make only a tiny mistake, he could become a totally different goalie. He would go from a keeper who could save flying missiles from any height and any direction, to someone who found it hard to even get a grip on a bouncing ball at low speed.

I realized someone needed to help him get over this complex he had, not only for his own sake, but that of the team too. So after a game one day I just approached him and said bluntly:

"Jamie, please listen to what I have to say. There is nothing you can do to undo a mistake on the field, so you have to stop beating yourself up each and every time something doesn't go your way.

The sooner you can let things go and push on with the game, the better it will be for both you and the rest of the team. I don't wish to sound harsh, but I felt something had to be said if we're to perform well as a team."

He looked at me and asked how he was supposed to forget making a stupid mistake and play on as if nothing had happened. I responded by telling him about the "pause for thought" strategy.

"Jamie, the next time a mistake happens, try closing your eyes for 10 seconds, then take a couple of deep breaths and tell yourself - with conviction - that whatever just happened no longer matters because it can't be undone."

Anyway, during the next game he made another goalkeeping blunder, albeit a minor one. I watched closely for his response, and instead of going into the all too familiar strop, I saw him immediately close his eyes and follow through with my suggested technique for overcoming mistakes.

After the game he told me what he had done, and how it really helped him come to terms with his disappointing performance at that moment.

He said that he was skeptical at first, but as there was nothing to lose by trying, he decided to test this approach and was so glad now that he did.

The lesson to take away from this is that crying over spilt milk is not going to do you or your team any favors.

What's done cannot be undone, so the sooner you accept this fact, the better it is for all concerned.

Simply use the pause for thought strategy with eyes closed, and you will get to see your disappointment magically disappear.

This approach to overcoming failure will undoubtedly help you develop into a smarter, more resilient goalie.

36 SHERIFF OF THE PENALTY AREA

I have touched on this topic earlier in the book. If you read the previous chapters, then you probably remember that I stressed the importance of being the sheriff inside your penalty box. We're now going to take a closer look at what it actually means in practice to be the one in charge of this area.

Well, as the goalkeeper, once the opponents enter your penalty box, you need to have them realize that you will not allow them to behave in here as they might do elsewhere on the field.

You should not show any mercy to your opponents in this area, and do everything you can to either grip, parry, or clear the ball away; it really doesn't matter which method you use. So long as you prevent the challengers from scoring, then you have done your job.

The more you are able to demonstrate authority and skill in the box, the more respect you will gain from the opponents. If you get known for being top dog in the penalty area, then your rivals will think twice before going for the ball here because they know you will be merciless.

OK, so just how do you actually become the "sheriff" of your penalty area if you don't really have the confidence to play in this way? Well, here are few pointers that will surely help you gain such authority:

-   Begin by shouting loud and making yourself heard. Once the opponents hear you they will quickly realize that they're entering your territory and that you are ready for them.

-   Avoid standing on the goal line as your opponents enter the penalty box; instead move toward them with confidence (fake it till you make it if you have to), as this will add pressure to their approach and also make you appear big.

-   Surprise the opponent by attacking him as soon as he enters the penalty box. Do this instead of taking the cautious approach by waiting for him to make his move with the ball.

-   Don't hesitate to sacrifice yourself in 50/50 situations. Remember, it is you who needs to show your opponents that you fear no man.

-   Make sure to act with authority and confidence (again, fake it till you make it if you have to) once you have the ball in your possession. Having, or appearing to have, self-assurance will show the opponent that you are prepared to do anything and everything to prevent him getting any free scoring opportunities.

-   Although you must not play unfair, or try to deliberately injure your opponent, you should, however, let it be known that things might hurt a bit for any challenger who dares to face you inside your penalty area.

-   Work at maintaining full control of the ball once it's passed over to you and don't, whatever you do, let an opponent's attempts to stress you out affect your game.

As you can see, there are a good few things that you can do to get comfortable with acting like the boss man in your penalty area.

You must always bear in mind that once the opponent enters the penalty line, then they are moving into dangerous territory. It is then that you need to act immediately and show them who is in charge here!

Finally, if any of the above tactics still make you uncomfortable and go against your natural grain, just fake it till you make it.

Push through your comfort zone no matter what! Believe me when I say, it won't be too long before you're playing the role of sheriff with renewed confidence.

37 HYDRATING YOUR BODY

It's an unfortunate fact, but most keepers don't realize the importance of hydration. Seriously, when any player is not hydrated properly it negatively impacts his performance.

The biggest mistake that most amateur goalies make is to only drink water when they feel thirsty. This is a bad strategy!

Waiting until you are parched could mean you are already becoming dehydrated.

There are three main ways in which the human body loses water. About 50% is lost in urine, 25% in respiration, and 25% through sweat, although the latter obviously increases with physical exertion. Some players are heavy spitters too, which is yet another channel where water is lost.

When the body loses water it's crucial that you replace those lost fluids to prevent dehydration. If you don't, then you will notice a steady decline in your performance.

This is because water helps to regulate the body's temperature, but furthermore, it moves nutrients necessary for energy, and also lubricates your joints.

There are several side effects that you can experience as a goalkeeper when you are not properly hydrated.

Some of these include poor muscular function, an inability to concentrate and focus on your tasks, and also a chance of collapsing (something I have witnessed) if you become too dehydrated.

At best you will feel lethargic to some degree depending on how much water your body has actually lost.

One easy way to find out whether you are, or are becoming dehydrated, is to inspect your urine.

If it's quite yellow or borderline orange and smells pungent, then you really need to drink some water as you are not sufficiently hydrated. Worth noting is the darker the pee, the more you need to drink.

On the other hand, if your urine is clear or just a faint yellow, and doesn't smell strong, then you are just fine!

The amount of water you should actually drink on game day can depend on your size, how much you sweat, and the position played.

For example, midfielders do the most running in a soccer game so they will probably lose the most amount of fluid.

But as a general guide, the recommended intake is about 2-3 liters of water per day for adults, and no more than 1-1.5 liters for kids.

However, there is a pitfall that you need to avoid, and one that many goalkeepers tend to fall into: DON'T drink the entire recommended amount of water in one hit, especially just prior to the start of a game.

Gulping down too much water too quickly is something that you must avoid doing at all cost. In fact, putting too much water into the body too soon can, in some cases, result in serious health issues if you are not careful.

In order to stay on the safe side, divide the daily recommended intake into equal portions and then consume it over the course of the day.

To give you an example, you get a 500ml reusable water bottle (don't reuse disposable plastic water bottles) that you re-fill every 2-3 hours.

Assume that the game is on during the late afternoon and that you start your day by getting up at 07:00 a.m.

You would then fill this bottle with 500ml, drink it slowly during the next 2-3 hours, and then repeat the same process until the recommended amount has been consumed.

In my experience, water is by far the best liquid for hydrating the body, and I suggest you to stay well away from any kind of sports drink, despite what the hype might promote on the label.

These types of drinks are often filled with all kinds of things your body doesn't need, plus they are expensive as well. Save your money and drink good clean drinking water instead!

To summarize this chapter: I want to stress the importance of proper hydration. This is something that will either make or break your performance on match day.

Don't fall into the trap that so many amateurs do by allowing your body to become even mildly dehydrated before a match. If in doubt, check your urine.

38 PREGAME RELAXING

One of the best kept secrets to goalkeeping success is to learn the art of relaxation. Knowing how to relax properly before a game can do wonders for your mental performance.

The idea behind this is to charge your body with positive energy and boost your confidence levels before you even get to make that first save.

The secret behind this is learning how to relax without complicating issues. There are certainly plenty of methods out there that are used to help players prepare mentally for the upcoming game, but many of these are overly complex, whereas my strategy is far from rocket science.

What you do is simply lie down on your bed, close your eyes, and put on some relaxing music of your choosing.

Once comfortable, visualize your success on the soccer field. Imagine yourself being an unbeatable keeper; one who can save any ball from any angle, no matter how many shots your opponent's fire at you!

To help you out I have created a small methodical checklist below that I recommend you follow, at least until you've compiled one of your own.

It's pretty straightforward, but I know from firsthand experience that it works really well providing you follow each of these steps and focus hard on getting the most of this technique.

1. Create a playlist of 10 songs on your computer, iPod, mp3 player, or whatever you use for playing music. Now start the first song.

2. Dim the lighting in your room if you can (you can use a sleep mask to block out the light if your room's too bright), then lie down on the bed and close your eyes. Get yourself into a nice relaxed state.

3. Now start visualizing yourself playing like a true champion. Observe your opponents faces and witness their pure frustration as your spectacular goalkeeping skills save one shot after another. Today, on this day, nothing can get past you.

4. Create whatever successful scenarios you want to for as long as the music is playing. The outcome is always in your hands, and the outcome is always in your favor.

It might be a good idea to make sure everyone in the house knows not to disturb during these sessions, so you might just want to have a word before you begin.

This is a simple example of how you can relax before a game. This undemanding technique not only calms you down, but it also gives you a boost of positive energy.

If you have never done anything like this before, then you're in for a treat. Honestly, you will be amazed how relaxed and prepared you feel afterwards.

Most amateur keepers think little about relaxing before a match, whereas a professional goalie understands just how important this is.

That's why you will often see great goalkeepers enter the stadium wearing headphones or earbuds.

If you are serious about your goalkeeping then you should really be doing this relax & energize exercise before your practice sessions as well.

By making this an integral part of your overall routine, you will juiced up and ready to roll even for training, and that can only help accelerate your development.

To summarize this chapter; I would like to end this section by emphasizing how important relaxation is for your mental performance, which consequently has a positive impact on your physical performance too.

Understand the true benefits of pre-match relaxation and exploit this simple technique.

Follow through on your new commitment and you will get to see yourself start to play like a true professional!

39 TALENT IS NOT ENOUGH

Just because a competing team member happens to be more talented than you, that doesn't necessarily mean he will immediately be chosen as the one to stand in goal.

It is really important to understand that talent is just one tool in the goalkeeper's toolkit, and if it's not maintained properly, then it alone will be of little use.

You can be someone who has an average talent and yet performs better than someone who's considered a highly gifted keeper.

The key here is to work twice as hard as that goalie to make up for your lack of "natural" talent.

Being naturally gifted is not worth much if the individual isn't prepared to sacrifice himself and work at maintaining and improving his skills.

That's right, even natural talent requires work if it's to be preserved.

During my college years, I was playing for a highly competitive team.

Most other teams in the area only had one goalie, but we were fortunate in that we had three good keepers competing for the goalie spot.

Two of these guys were more talented than the other. The least talented of the three still showed promise on practice days, but he'd never actually played in goal during a real match.

This was obviously to his disadvantage, especially as we had two better players vying for the post who had plenty of real-world experience.

During the pre-season it was pretty obvious that one of the more talented players would get the top slot, and the less talented goalie would be spending most of time on the bench as a substitute keeper, just hoping to get an opportunity to play at some point.

In spite of what seemed like an inevitable outcome, this goalie simply refused to give up.

He was always the first one to arrive on practice days and the last one to leave. He worked incredibly hard during training too.

He did everything he possibly could to convince the coach that it was in the team's best interest to give him a break.

Then came a match day when both of the more experienced keepers were away; one with an injury and the other because of a commitment at school.

Our coach had no other choice but to allow the stand-in keeper to play in goal.

Well, to say he impressed us all would be a gross understatement.

From that game one, neither of the other two keepers was able to regain their place as the team's best option for goalie.

The coach was not only surprised at how far the third keeper had improved his game over the months, but he actually admitted that he'd become the better player, so much so that he decided to make him the number one goalie.

The other two keepers suddenly found themselves as second and third substitutes, and were forced to watch the rest of the season from the bench.

The following season the less talented, yet still better goalie, kept his number one spot.

The other two realized it would take a lot of work and effort to bring their talents back up to scratch and get a second chance at being first choice goalie.

Neither, it seemed, were prepared for that, so they both decided to quit the team and join another club.

The reason for reciting this story is to illustrate how hard work and commitment always pays off in the long term.

The two naturally talented keepers in this account had become a tad complacent, and because of that had let their game slip. Hard work, patience, and unrelenting perseverance will always beat talent when the talented one doesn't maintain his skills.

I've seen plenty of gifted goalies in my time throw away an opportunity for going professional, and why?

They were just not prepared to put in the hard work required to maintain and improve on the talent they already possessed.

They simply thought that talent alone would be enough to see them make the big time.

Most found out, typically when it was too late, that they thought wrong!

Obviously not all naturally talented players miss their calling.

I've also had the opportunity to witness other goalkeepers who were not naturally gifted make it into top teams.

These goalies had to work extra hard though, not only to become good at the job, but also to constantly maintain their skills once they acquired them.

To summarize this chapter: be mindful of the fact that with determination, focus, and hard work, you can reach just about any goal you've set yourself.

On the other hand, if you are naturally talented, don't rely solely on that. Instead, work hard every day to maintain what you're blessed with, and always strive to improve.

It doesn't matter how good you might be, there is always room to become even better.

Finally, heed the story above!

40 A DIFFERENT KIND OF WARM-UP

The warm up routine of a goalie must be completely different to that of the other players. The worst thing you can do is to just slip on the gloves and have your teammate's fire powerful shots at you if you've not warmed up, or have warmed up incorrectly.

Skipping a warm-up is inviting injury. It's really important to understand that because avoiding a pre-match or pre-game warm-up – which doesn't take long – could see you out of action for weeks, months, or even an entire season.

It's also important not to simply join in with the warm-up session that the other players do. At best, it won't do you any good, and at worse, it could result in hurt or serious harm because you won't have prepared yourself as a goalkeeper.

The problem with a goalie's warm-up session is that there is no standard. Most keepers tend to devise their own routine of what they do and how.

This means you will need to spend some time figuring out what works best for you and the way you play your game.

The best approach is to try several different routines and decide what suits you best.

For example, you might be one of those goalkeepers who need a really hard warm up in order to perform at your optimum.

On the other hand, you could be the complete opposite, but until you've researched this further you won't know.

I once trained with a goalkeeper who was actually not very good, or at least he never gave that impression during practice.

Anyhow, he was our only keeper so we had to accept him for what he was. We just hoped that he performed better during the forthcoming games than he did during practice sessions.

It was our first game of the season and I was put on the bench (that's another story for another book!). The coach told me to spend some time warming up with the goalie.

I can remember him saying that he'd like to try a different warm-up approach to the usual. This time he wanted to work hard during the warm-up as he had read somewhere that it helps goalies perform better.

I actually laughed when I heard that because I could not understand how a different warm up would help him perform better.

And anyway, a warm-up essentially involves "gentle" exercise or practice, so I wasn't convinced, but decided to go along with him nonetheless.

As the warm-up progressed he became really focused and determined with the task in hand. I actually saw sweat break through his shirt for the first time since I began practicing with him all those months ago.

Once the game started the disbelief kicked in. The way this guy performed was amazing, so much so that it was like watching a completely different keeper to the one we had gotten to know.

He continued to make one great save after another.

His performance was truly incredible and a joy to watch.

After this magnificent feat he was voted "player of the game." It was certainly a well-earned title, not to mention a total surprise.

I asked him, somewhat tongue in cheek, what he had been taking in order to perform so well.

He said that the key was in the pre-match warm-up, and on that note he just smiled at me and took to the showers.

At the next game he carried out the same warm-up routine and gave the same brilliant performance during the match, just like previously.

Game after game it was the same story. Needless to say, it wasn't too long before he got moved up to the first team.

This was obviously a blow for us because we had to take on another keeper, and this time, unfortunately, he was on the poor side of average!

I hope this shows you how important the warm up actually is for your game.

Not only is it crucial for reducing the chance of hurt or serious injury, but it can also improve your performance by several levels, providing of course, you just find the warm-up routine that works best for you.

41 NEVER BECOME SATISFIED

One of the big pitfalls that a lot of keepers get drawn into is that of fulfillment. A goalie, more so than any other team player, tends to get satisfied with his achievements and skills pretty quickly.

He reaches the conclusion that he's at the top of his game and does little or nothing to progress further as he assumes there's nowhere else to go.

This belief is pure fallacy and nothing could be further from the truth.

Getting to the top of your game is one thing, but staying there and improving still further is something that has to be worked at.

In order to remain at the top you need to work really hard as it can be a very slippery place. I've seen goalies reach their peak only to fall from grace a short time afterwards, most of whom would never regain their previous status.

The most successful keepers in the world did not get there because of coincidence. They got there because they never became complacent or treated their accomplishments as something that was set in stone.

These guys understand that improvement is always possible no matter how skilled one might happen be.

They constantly look for new ways to further enhance their abilities, and they never settle thinking they're at the top of their game with no place left to go.

When a goalie becomes satisfied with his skills and achievements, what he's actually doing is stunting his development.

Whenever development becomes limited, there is always a negative impact on performance.

Obviously, any drop in performance can cost the keeper a place on the team if those he is competing against (see chapter 39.) continue to work hard at their own game and subsequently become the better man for the job.

To illustrate how this can affect your development and performance, I will use the sport of boxing as a metaphor.

Although boxing as an activity doesn't have much in common with soccer, the mindset of a boxer can be drawn upon to help with your goalkeeping success.

As you probably know, a boxer must constantly be hungry for success, and never, not for a second, take his eye of the goal (in this case the fight).

Whenever a boxer loses focus, even ever so slightly, the time is fast approaching where he will need to hang up the gloves. Those who keep on top of their game are hungry for success – relentlessly – and totally committed to winning.

This highly controlled mental approach keeps them at the top of their game and they remain there for the rest of their boxing career.

As a goalkeeper, you need to adopt the same mental approach as these boxers.

Get hungry for success and stay hungry; don't allow anyone, or anything, to get in your way.

You can be pretty sure of one thing: if you ever do reach the point of self-satisfaction and lose that strong determination to constantly improve and succeed, then it's game up!

From that point on it will only be a matter of time before you fall off your throne and lose that crowning glory you once had.

There is nothing new or advanced in this way of thinking, yet it's all too easy to discard or forget about. I just want you to know that acquiring the right attitude is half the battle.

By having the proper mindset you will, without any question or doubt, develop and perform much quicker and a lot better as a goalkeeper.

To summarize this chapter: Make sure you never become satisfied with your skill level and achievements.

Remember that it was true grit and a hunger to succeed that got you to where you are. It will be that same grit and hunger for more of the same that keeps you on top of your game.

42 PARRY OR NOT TO PARRY!

Parrying is a term used when a ball is sent high or wide by pinching or using the fingertips to push it away.

This technique is often used if the ball is beyond reach for a definite catch. Parrying is best executed in situations where you are not absolutely sure a good catch is possible.

A common mistake made by inexperienced keepers is to try catching the ball when they should in fact parry it.

A professional keeper knows exactly when he should parry the ball whereas an amateur will usually do everything he can to catch it. This can often result in a goal, especially if the opponents are smart enough to lure close to the ball.

The question is to know when to parry and when to attempt a catch. The general rule of thumb is this: if you have any doubts, no matter how slight, you should parry the ball. Just one little mistake here can devastate your entire performance.

There may be other circumstances that help decide whether to parry the ball instead of catch it. It's impossible to list them all, of course, so I will stick to the most common one's and explain how they affect your decision to parry or not:

- **Rainy weather**: During wet weather, the ball is going to be really slippery and difficult to grip. It is therefore better to try parrying more during rainy days.
- **Powerful shot**: If you face a powerful shot from a short distance, then it's always better to parry the ball rather than make an attempt to grip it. This is because a failed catch can easily cause a rebound, thus giving an opponent a goal scoring opportunity.
- **Looming opponents**: In my experience, it's better to parry the ball when you have a lot of opponents within close proximity as your chances of getting a good, clean grip with so many threats nearby are diminished.

The three points above are just a few examples, but there are many other scenarios.

However, these should give you a general idea of situations where it's better to parry.

Now, I want to tell you a story about how making a wrong decision can destroy an otherwise awesome performance, and explain why parrying should be your first option when in doubt.

During my college years I played in a team that was made up of some the best players in our region. We had one of the finest goalkeepers in the district and he was able to save shots that you wouldn't even think were savable.

However, despite his obvious skill and impressive dexterity in goal, he wasn't totally flawless.

His main weakness was his inability to know when best to parry the ball and when to grip it.

During the most important game of the season, he saved two penalties and also performed several great saves during the match.

Despite an overall impressive performance, the goalie made just one silly mistake that cost us the game.

What he did was attempt to catch a shot that he should have parried. All his amazing saves throughout the match amounted to nothing now as they were destroyed by this one blunder.

That might sound a little unfair, but it's the reality of the situation and one of the disappointments that can come from being a goalkeeper.

It is one thing losing simply because the other team played a better game, but no one likes to lose because of an avoidable gaffe.

What you should learn from this story is the fact that you must always parry a shot whenever you are in doubt about it. It's just not worth the risk of losing a game from a simple misjudgment.

To summarize this chapter: Try to remember this one thing: you can make great saves throughout the entire game and be the star of the match, but all it takes is one simple gaff and everything else you've done before becomes insignificant, or certainly less momentous.

Letting in a goal because it was a fantastic shot will not diminish your efforts, but an error of judgment just might. Again, if in doubt as to parry or not, always err on the side of caution and parry!

43 INTERPRETING SHOOTING FROM SHORT DISTANCE

Being able to interpret your opponent's intentions is very important as it will determine how many goals you let in, or not, depending how good at it you are.

The better you can become at reading your challengers, the more likely you will be able to save the shot.

This is because you will get know exactly how and where to dive at that crucial moment.

I've noticed over time how most soccer players tend to point their supporting foot in the direction of where they indent to shoot. They also tend to glance in the direction of the strike too, just prior to releasing the shot.

Reading the intentions of your opponents is even more important when they are about to shoot from short distances (less than 10 yards).

Here, your ability to interpret the shot will often decide whether you get to save it or are forced to relent.

I know from experience that players rarely have time to fire a controlled shot when they are short on time.

Instead, they just kick the ball in the right direction and hope for the best. In situations like these, you have an ideal opportunity to save the attempt if you interpret the shot correctly.

To help master this skill, I suggest you try a somewhat unpopular strategy which is to play a few games as an outfield player.

By doing this you will be able to get into the mindset of an outfield player, which is something you should then be able to turn to your advantage when standing back in goal.

I'm telling you this because several years ago I was playing with a goalkeeper who was incredibly good at interpreting shots from short distances.

It was as if he could get into the minds of his opponents and find out firsthand where they intended to shoot.

After one of the games I was so curious to discover his secret that I just came out and asked him how he was able to perform one amazing save after another, whereas I could barely see where the ball was coming from half the time.

He looked at me, winked, and simply said: "I was not always a goalkeeper."

He explained that in his previous team he was sometimes forced to be an outfield player because they had two keepers, but were short of other players.

By playing outfield, he explained how he got invaluable knowledge on how players responded in certain situations. In other words, he got to know what it is that makes an outfield player tick.

He also wanted to emphasize the fact that he only played outfield for few games, but it was enough for him to understand the mindset of these players.

He then used this newfound knowledge to his own advantage when he was back playing in goal.

The lesson you should take from this is that you should try playing few games as an outfield player yourself and then evaluate the experience.

There's a pretty good chance you will be able to take what you learn and use it to your own advantage.

By doing this one exercise you might get to move your game up to a whole new level, and then you too will become someone who is able to make fantastic saves from short distance shooting, just like the keeper above.

44 DISTANCE FROM THE POSTS

Keeping a proper distance from the posts is one of the fundamentals skills you will learn as a goalie. You must always know where your exact position is on the goal line and monitor your distance from the left and right posts.

No matter how talented you are, you still need to pay attention to this skill because it can save you a lot of humiliation on the field. To illustrate its importance, I will tell you about a time where a good goalie's attempt at a save went badly wrong simply because he wasn't aware of his position on the goal line.

A few years ago I was watching a game where the best players from our district where playing against another region. This was a game where the coaches got to decide who would get to the regional cup (where the selection for the national team is made).

I'd heard a lot of talk about one goalie who was admired for his amazing reflexes and ability to read the game. I was certainly eager to see him play since as he was so highly acclaimed by those who knew, or knew of him. Once the match began, I couldn't help but notice how this keeper had problems with positioning himself properly on the goal line.

He often left huge open gaps to the right; something I found odd considering he was supposed to be the best, or one of the best goalies in the region.

There was one situation where an opponent was clearly preparing to fire a powerful shot. The goalkeeper positioned himself about two yards to the left, leaving a whopping six yard gap to the right. The coach was yelling from the sideline, but the keeper either didn't hear or refused to listen.

As the shot was fired to the right he dived for the ball, but the inevitable happened! He landed at least three yards short of the right post and a goal was scored.

Immediately after that, a disgruntled coach took him off the field. This goalie had just blown any chance he might have had of playing in the regional cup. Because of this blunder, a replacement goalkeeper now got a crack of bettering his own career.

By all accounts, the sent-off goalie was really good, but because of this one flaw in his game, he was not good enough when it mattered most. In order to avoid the same destiny as him, you should always try to monitor your distance from the posts.

It's a good idea to study professional keepers to see how they perform in these situations. You will notice how when an opponent approaches the goal with the intention to shoot, the goalie quickly glances over to his left and right so as to determine his exact position on the goal line.

In the majority of cases this is little more than a last minute spot check. Most of the time, a professional keeper will already be positioned properly because of his instincts.

Even so, a quick last minute check avoids making the mistake of being too far from one of the posts at that crucial movement. The tactic is simple, and may well seem logical, but many an amateur goalie has been defeated by a less than average shot because he ignored this simple rule.

ENDING...

My last advice to you is following: If you have a dream, then do not give it up just because someone says that you will not make it and remember to always believe in yourself no matter what!